Handbook for Planning an Effective Writing Program

Kindergarten Through Grade Twelve

1986 Edition

Publishing Information

The *Handbook for Planning an Effective Writing Program* was prepared by the Handbook Writing Committee under the direction of George F. Nemetz, Consultant in English, California State Department of Education. (See the Acknowledgments for a list of committee members.) Mr. Nemetz also directed the preparation of the 1983 and 1986 revised editions of the handbook. The handbook was edited by Theodore R. Smith and prepared for photo-offset production by the staff of the Bureau of Publications, California State Department of Education. The artwork and design for the 1982 and 1986 editions were prepared by Steve Yee; and for the 1983 edition, by Cheryl Shawver McDonald. The document was published by the Department of Education, 721 Capitol Mall, Sacramento, California (mailing address: P.O. Box 944272, Sacramento, CA 94244-2720); it was printed by the Office of State Printing and distributed under the provisions of the Library Distribution Act and *Government Code* Section 11096.

Copies of this publication are available for $2.50 each, plus sales tax for California residents, from Publications Sales, California State Department of Education, P.O. Box 271, Sacramento, CA 95802-0271.

A list of other publications available from the Department may be found on page 69 of this handbook.

ISBN 0-8011-0290-1

EDITOR'S NOTE: Those who developed this handbook followed all eight stages in the writing process, which are described on pages 11 through 24 of the document. The editing stage, as described on page 19, was composed of these tasks: (1) adhering to the rules of the language and a recognized style; (2) using good diction; (3) following logical syntax; (4) making the text and its references accurate; (5) developing a good format; and (6) proofreading at each step in the process of preparing the manuscript for printing. In addition to the references cited on pages 19 and 20 of this handbook, the editor used *Webster's New Collegiate Dictionary* and *Webster's Third New International Dictionary* to resolve any questions regarding preferred spelling and syllabication. The Bureau of Publications has developed its own style for footnotes and bibliographical entries; thus, the editor did not use *The Chicago Manual of Style* as a guide for such entries, but he did use that stylebook as a guide for resolving other matters of style and for preparing the index, which he added to the 1983 revised edition of the handbook.

To achieve good readability, the editor had the text set on a maximum line length of 15 picas in 11-point Times Roman type, and he had one point of leading added between each line of type. The headings for each section of the handbook were set in 30-point Times boldface type. The material in the appendix was set in 10-point type, and the footnotes, this note, and the index were set in 8-point type. The typesetter, Leatrice Shimabukuro, used a computerized phototypesetting machine and magnetic disks for composing the manuscript.

The sidebars, which appear in the margins of the handbook, were selected by George Nemetz and the editor to highlight as many of the central ideas of the text as it was possible to emphasize. In addition, the format was designed to capture the spirit of the writing process and to complement the text. To achieve the desired graphic effect, the artists made high contrast prints of the photographs and screened them to 60 percent of their original intensity.

In 1984 the Educational Press Association of America awarded the handbook and its preparers distinguished achievement awards in recognition of the quality of the writing, editing, and graphics in the document.

T.R.S.

EDPRESS

Contents

"The limits of my language stand for the limits of my world."
Ludwig Wittgenstein

Foreword

As a people who value the lessons of history, we must realize that our very survival depends primarily on our collective abilities to speak and write clearly and precisely and to be understood as we strive to understand others.

I am convinced of the power of language, of its necessity to our lives, and of its vital role in education. I am equally convinced of the consequences to our society if we are imprecise or illogical in our use of language and if we ignore its beauty or debase its heritage. I am so convinced of this that I propose here, as I have in the past, to give the highest possible priority to helping all who are involved in education—teachers, students, school administrators, parents—gain the language skills they need to communicate well. Without such skills—listening, speaking, reading, writing—our students and educators alike remain crippled in whatever they attempt to do.

I believe that through our language, in all its forms, we maintain our position of highest order in the animal kingdom. With that same language, we define ourselves as we are and what we hope to be. It is through what we say and what we write that we maintain our history as a civilized society. Language is our link with both the past and the future—with who we were and who we will inevitably be. As a people who value the lessons of history, we must realize that our very survival depends primarily on our collective abilities to speak and write clearly and precisely and to be understood as we strive to understand others.

This handbook was prepared in the light of the centrality of language in our lives. I know that the effort to help students learn to speak and write with facility is one of the most difficult tasks teachers face. However, I also know that most teachers have not been well prepared to teach writing. Although they may be very knowledgeable in specific subject matter areas, most teachers do not know how to elicit good student writing—do not know the stages of the writing process. In fact, I have noted that many teachers seem to be afraid to write and, thus, cannot serve as models for their students. This is largely true because, until recently, writing simply was not emphasized in most teacher preparation programs.

Obviously, staff development programs for planning and establishing good writing programs are needed, and this handbook was developed to facilitate that. If it is used properly, the handbook can be a valuable tool for those wishing to assess the quality of a school's writing program, to pinpoint the needs for staff development, and to plan and implement a new program.

In providing for effective staff development in the teaching of writing, we in California are fortunate because of the emergence in 1974 of the University of California, Berkeley/Bay Area Writing Project. I have followed its development from the beginning, and I have given my wholehearted support to efforts to expand it to other sites in the state. We now have 19 such sites, and the statewide effort has become known as the California Writing Project, which is described in Appendix B.

I believe the California Writing Project is one of the most effective staff development efforts for improving the teaching of writing. Its emergence was most timely, and I hope that this handbook will be useful not only for those trained through the project but also for all others who need help in planning and carrying out staff development programs in this curricular area.

Several of those who worked on this publication are associated with the California Writing Project. Thus, many of the ideas in the handbook reflect the eminent practicality and effectiveness of that project. I congratulate those who worked on this document for producing what I believe is one of the most useful tools I have ever encountered for helping educators develop effective programs for the teaching of writing.

Bill Honig

Superintendent of Public Instruction

"I don't know what I think until I see what I've said."

E. M. Forster

> *"Writing is the basic stuff of education. It has been sorely neglected in our schools."*
>
> *Donald H. Graves*

Acknowledgments

This handbook was prepared with the help of a group of educators who are highly informed regarding the teaching and learning of writing. Many of them are associated with writing centers that make up the California Writing Project and were nominated to serve on the Writing Handbook Committee by the directors of those centers. Others on the committee were selected on the basis of their expertise in specific areas.

As might be expected, spirited dialogue occurred during committee meetings because of the vantage points of the different committee members. However, they were able to reach consensus, and this handbook represents a distillation of the discussions, writing, and rewriting in which they engaged. It also reflects the suggestions and contributions from a large group of reviewers of early drafts.

The members of the Handbook Writing Committee follow, and the Department of Education is particularly grateful for all of their contributions to the development of the handbook:

Sheila Anchondo, District Resource Teacher, San Bernardino City Unified School District

Beverly R. Banks, Writing Project Director, Kern Union High School District, Bakersfield

Roberta A. Beatty, Teacher/Writing Coordinator, Beverly Hills High School, Beverly Hills Unified School District

Betty Bivins, Secondary English Adviser, Area 10 Instructional Services Office, Los Angeles Unified School District

Yetive J. Bradley, Reading/Language Consultant, Oakland Unified School District

Gerald Camp, Teacher, Fremont Union High School District, Sunnyvale

Karen A. Carlton, Instructor, Humboldt State University, Arcata

Marcialyn J. Carter, Arroyo Grande High School, Lucia Mar Unified School District

Mary Frances Everhart, Instructor, City College of San Francisco

Myron Flindt, Teacher, Ponderosa Elementary School, Paradise Unified School District

Martha Johnson, Instructor, Study Skills Center, San Diego State University

George Lober, Jr., Teacher, Clovis High School, Clovis Unified School District

Miriam Ojeda, Associate Professor, Department of Chicano Studies, California State University, Northridge

Glenn F. Patchell, Teacher, Irvine High School, Irvine Unified School District

William J. Rice, English Teacher, Independence High School, East Side Union High School District, San Jose

Suzanne Sekula, Learning Center Assessment Specialist, Santa Monica College

Linda L. Wiezorek, Los Berros Elementary School, Lompoc Unified School District

Elizabeth Wood, Fellow, South Coast Writing Project, University of California, Santa Barbara

George F. Nemetz, Consultant to the Committee and Project Coordinator; Consultant in English, California State Department of Education

The principal writer for the first edition of this handbook was Professor Eugene Soules of the English Department of Sonoma State University. The footnotes and selected references were compiled by committee members Elizabeth Wood and Gerald Camp. Significant help in writing the section on the needs of language minority students was provided by Eleanor Thonis of the Wheatland School District and by Fred Dobb, Dennis Parker, and Rosario Pineyro-Ostby of the State Department of Education. Other members of the Department who provided assistance were Elizabeth Breneman, Phil Daro, Mae Gundlach, Bruce Hagen, Joseph Hoffmann, Donavan Merck, Jill Neeley, Robert Ryan, Emanuel Scrofani, James Smith, and Robert Tardif.

The section on the use of computers in writing was added to the 1983 revised edition of the handbook, and George Nemetz and Theodore Smith consulted with the following persons in preparing the material and in selecting appropriate entries on computers for the Selected References: Thomas Gage, Humboldt State University; G. William King, University of California, Davis; Stephen Marcus, University of California, Santa Barbara; and Owen Thomas, University of California, Irvine.

In preparing material for the 1986 edition of this handbook, George Nemetz received special help and contributions from Sheridan Blau of the University of California, Santa Barbara; Elizabeth Breneman, State Department of Education; Eugene Soules, Sonoma State Uni-

versity; and Iris Tiedt, San Jose State University. Also, Stephen Marcus of the University of California, Santa Barbara, and author of "The Muse and the Machine," which appeared in the 1983 edition of the handbook, suggested that the article be replaced with "Computers in the Curriculum," which appeared in the October, 1984, edition of *Electronic Learning.* The publishers of the *Electronic Learning,* Scholastic, Inc., granted permission for us to reproduce the article, and it appears in Appendix C.

Credits for Photographs

Several of the photographs appearing in this publication, including the one on this page, were taken by Kim Hicks at one of the "Writing in the 80's" workshops, which were held in 1982 and 1983 to introduce this handbook and the latest ideas in the teaching of writing to the educational community in California. Ms. Hicks is employed by the office of the Orange County Superintendent of Schools. Kenneth S. Lane of the University of California, Berkeley, also took many of the photographs used in the handbook. The Department acknowledges not only the work of both Ms. Hicks and Mr. Lane but also the following photographers and organizations for the other photos used throughout the document: American National Red Cross; Jackie Berman, Writer-Photographer, *School Improvement Exchange;* Aaron D. Freeman, Yorba Linda; Los Nietos School District; Sylvia Olds; Rondal Partridge; Sacramento City Unified School District; San Diego City Schools; San Juan Unified School District; Kazuhiro Tsuruta, San Francisco; and Carol Wheeler, Media Services Unit, Department of Education.

"Several of those who worked on this handbook are associated with the California Writing Project. Thus, many of the ideas in the handbook reflect the eminent practicality and effectiveness of that project."

Bill Honig

Preface

One of the major missions of the California State Department of Education in the 1980s is to provide leadership and assistance to those persons and local agencies that are working to improve the instructional programs in our schools. As Superintendent Bill Honig has said, "We will shift the emphasis in the Department from bureaucratic processes, such as the reading of plans, to the provision of substantive assistance in curriculum and instruction." The production of curriculum handbooks, such as this one on writing, supports Superintendent Honig's mission for the Department.

This handbook and those that have been prepared in other curricular areas are addressed to those individuals and groups that wish to review and improve educational programs. However, the documents are addressed more specifically to those persons at school site levels who plan and implement curricula.

The *Handbook for Planning an Effective Writing Program* was designed to provide schools with a standard for assessing the quality of their writing programs and for developing new improved programs when it is appropriate. Our intent is that the handbook augment, not supplant, other curriculum documents, such as the *Model Curriculum Standards,* the *English–Language Arts Framework for California Public Schools,* the *English–Language Arts Model Curriculum Guide,* the county superintendents' *Course of Study,* and locally developed planning and curriculum guides.

We are most grateful for the contributions, advice, and assistance provided by members of the committee that helped prepare the first edition of the handbook and those who helped with this revised version. We are also grateful for the suggestions and reactions of those who reviewed various drafts of the document. And we acknowledge the persistence and commitment of George F. Nemetz, who coordinated the entire effort.

We are especially pleased that this handbook, which is now in its fourth printing, has been so well received not only in California but also in other parts of the country. According to the Bureau of Publications, over 100,000 copies of this handbook are now in use, and in 1984 the Educational Press Association of America awarded the handbook and its preparers distinguished achievement awards in recognition of the quality of the writing, editing, and graphics in the document. Thus, all of those involved in the handbook's development and production can be justifiably proud of their creative efforts. In addition, those who conducted the very popular "Writing in the 80's" workshops are to be congratulated. It was in these workshops that educators were shown how to use the handbook most effectively.

We realize that the true value of all our efforts to improve student writing may not be known for some time, but all of the signposts indicate that we are on the right road, and it is most gratifying to be there.

JAMES R. SMITH
Deputy Superintendent, Curriculum and Instructional Leadership

FRANCIE ALEXANDER
Director, Curriculum, Instruction, and Assessment Division

DONAVAN MERCK
Manager, Language Arts and Foreign Languages Unit

This handbook and those that have been prepared in other curricular areas are addressed to those individuals and groups that wish to review and improve educational programs.

I. Introduction to the Handbook

The Purpose of the Handbook

This handbook was designed to provide the schools of California with a standard for assessing their existing writing programs and a tool for helping them design new programs. Thus, the intended audience for the publication includes all those people at the school level who have responsibilities for planning curricula. However, in addition to curriculum specialists, teachers, and school administrators, the audience also includes school site councils, parents, and students responsible for planning writing programs.

School-level planners will find the handbook helpful in identifying the strengths and weaknesses of existing or proposed writing programs and in selecting strategies for change. The writers of the handbook have addressed both the content and teaching methodology of a writing program; that is, what ought to be taught and how. The discussion of each writing component includes a narrative and suggested activities, which are adaptable to various grade levels. However, readers are urged to add their own ideas to these lists of suggestions, thereby making the handbook more immediately useful to them. A list of selected references appears at the end of the handbook, and suggestions for further reading appear throughout the document.

Since the handbook's writers focus primarily on the components of a writing program, those desiring more information regarding the broad curriculum of English may wish to consult the *English Language Arts Framework for California Public Schools,* a publication of the California State Department of Education. However, it should be emphasized that this handbook is intended to complement, not supplant, the framework. While the handbook is consistent with the framework, its purpose differs.

The users of this handbook will also find another Department publication most useful. *Practical Ideas for Teaching Writing as a Process,* which came off the presses early in 1986, is a collection of specific classroom strategies and suggestions for teaching writing according to the process outlined in this handbook. The new book, which had its beginning in the California Writing Project at the University of California, Irvine, is the brainchild of Carol Booth Olson, codirector of that project. Each chapter of the new book begins with an essay by an authority in the field of English education in which the person presents a strategy for teaching writing as a process. Each essay is followed by specific classroom techniques for employing the strategy, and these were written by teachers who have used the techniques successfully in their classes. (For information on ordering the new book, see the Selected Publications of the Department of Education at the end of this handbook.)

Basic Principles of an Effective Writing Program

An effective writing program:

- Is a schoolwide effort involving writing as a means of learning in all curricular areas
- Provides a wide range of writing experiences for learning in all subject matter areas
- Builds on students' interests and on their reading and oral language experiences
- Offers the opportunity for students at any level to develop *fluency* before they are overly burdened with the fear of error, but with the expectation that they will later attain mastery of form and correctness (*Fluency,* as used here and elsewhere in this document, means the ease and confidence with which a writer is able to put thoughts on paper. It is the facility for being able to write without the constraints and fear of error.)
- Provides for adequate "time on task," which is basic to the learning process
- Provides staff development for the instructional staff
- Helps students to discover that writing is a way of learning about one's self and about the world, of developing thinking

skills, of generating new ideas, and of helping one to survive in an increasingly dynamic and complicated society

An effective writing program treats *writing as a process,* a concept which regards the act of writing as an interrelated series of creative activities. Included within this series are prewriting, writing, responding, revising, editing, developing skills with the conventions of writing, evaluating, and postwriting. The process has several stages in which:

- All parts of the process are given appropriate attention.
- Instruction in specific skills is integrated into the writing process at appropriate points.
- Students write frequently.
- Students write in all subject areas.
- Students write in many modes, such as descriptive, narrative, persuasive, and so forth.
- Students write for a variety of audiences and purposes.
- Teachers serve as models by doing the same exercises they assign their students.

An effective writing program produces students who:

- Believe that what they have to say is important.
- Are motivated to write, because they feel they have something significant to say.
- Write fluently, coherently, and correctly and with economy of expression.
- Do not overly fear putting their ideas on paper for the consideration of others.
- Realize that composing is an important learning tool in all curricular areas.

An effective writing program is a schoolwide effort involving writing as a means of learning in all curricular areas.

- Are able to write in many modes and for a variety of audiences and purposes.
- Readily engage in revising and editing early drafts.
- Pursue the writing task without spending undue time "staring at a blank page."
- Evidence some enjoyment of the act of writing.

(NOTE: For further reading on the basic principles of an effective writing program, see the entries in the Selected References for James L. Kinneavy, James Moffett, and Lev Vygotsky; also see *Practical Ideas for Teaching Writing as a Process.*)

Review of Research on the Teaching of Writing

The basic question the writers of this handbook attempted to answer is "What are the components of an effective writing program?" While the suggestions in the handbook are based on research of teaching practices that have contributed to improvement in writing abilities, they are also based on the professional backgrounds and experiences of the handbook's writers and reviewers. Although many practices merit additional research, much is already known about which practices in teaching the writing process are effective.[1] Since several of these findings are in conflict with widespread practices in the schools, both the effective and ineffective practices are identified here:

- *Grammar.* Perhaps the most widely ignored research finding is that the teaching of formal grammar, if divorced from the process of writing, has little or

no effect on the writing ability of students.[2] Studies from 1906 through 1976 have repeatedly reached this conclusion.[3] It seems to make no difference whether the system taught is traditional, structural, or transformational grammar.[4][5] Such instruction, when not directly related with the writing process, does not help students improve their writing.[6]

Furthermore, some researchers have concluded that in programs in which excessive time is devoted to the study of grammar independently of the writing process, the effects are negative. They have found that the quality of writing

Much is already known about which practices in teaching the writing process are effective.

[1]Elizabeth F. Haynes, "Using Research in Preparing to Teach Writing," *English Journal,* Vol. 67 (January, 1978), 82—88.

[2]Wilbur W. Hatfield, *An Experience Curriculum in English.* A Report of the Curriculum Commission, National Council of Teachers of English. New York: D. Appleton-Century Co., 1935, p. 228.

[3]Ingrid M. Strom, *Research in Grammar and Usage and Its Implications for Teaching Writing,* Bulletin of the School of Education, Indiana University, Vol. 36, No. 5 (September, 1960), 13-14.

[4]Stephen J. Sherwin, *Four Problems in Teaching English: A Critique of Research.* Scranton, Penn.: International Textbook Co., 1969, p. 156.

[5]W. B. Elley and others, "The Role of Grammar in a Secondary School English Curriculum," *Research in the Teaching of English,* Vol. 10 (spring, 1976), 17-18.

[6]Richard Braddock and others, *Research in Written Composition.* Urbana, Ill.: National Council of Teachers of English, 1963, p. 83.

of students enrolled in such programs not only does not improve but may even decline.[7] This is not to say that the study of grammar has no place in a writing program. A knowledge of the conventions of the writing of standard English, including appropriate grammar and usage, is important to students, particularly when they edit and revise their writing. However, it is best taught when a specific need for it emerges in a student's writing, not in isolation from actual writing. It is the latter approach to the teaching of grammar which is not supported by research.

- *Sentence combining.* Sentence combining is a technique for combining short sentences into longer, carefully constructed sentences. Over the past ten years, several studies of classes from the elementary school level through the first year in college have shown that sentence-combining exercises, both oral and written, even when conducted with little or no grammatical terminology, can be effective in increasing the sentence-writing maturity of students.[8] [9] [10]

The act of writing, in and of itself, does not necessarily improve the quality of a student's writing.

- *Quantity.* The act of writing, in and of itself, does not necessarily improve the quality of a student's writing. That is, just increasing the number of writing opportunities without providing appropriate instruction and other learning opportunities does not, in and of itself, result in a significant improvement of students' writing skills.[11] [12] [13] [14]

- *Response.* On the other hand, some research indicates that writing which includes responses from peers or teachers produces superior results. Response, the reader's reaction to a piece of writing, appears to be what makes quantity effective.[15] [16] (See page 16 in this handbook for a description of responding as one of the steps in the writing process.)

[7]Herbert J. Muller, *The Uses of English: Guides for the Teaching of English from the Anglo-American Conference at Dartmouth College.* New York: Holt, Rinehart and Winston, Inc., 1967, p. 102.

[8]Frank O'Hare, *Sentence-Combining: Improving Student Writing Without Formal Grammar Instruction,* Urbana, Ill.: National Council of Teachers of English, 1973, pp. 57, 68.

[9]Charles Cooper, "Research Roundup: Oral and Written Composition," *English Journal,* Vol. 64 (December, 1975), 72.

[10]John C. Mellon, *Transformational Sentence-Combining: A Method for Enhancing the Development of Syntactic Fluency in English Composition,* NCTE Research Report No. 10. Urbana, Ill.: National Council of Teachers of English, 1969, pp. 35, 71, 74.

[11]Paul Dressel and others, "The Effect of Writing Frequency Upon Essay-Type Writing Proficiency at the College Level," *Journal of Educational Research,* Vol. 46 (December, 1952), 292.

[12]Frank Heys, Jr., "The Theme-a-Week Assumption: A Report of an Experiment," *English Journal,* Vol. 51 (May, 1962), 320, 322.

[13]Lois V. Arnold, "Writer's Cramp and Eyestrain—Are They Paying Off?," *English Journal,* Vol. 53 (January, 1964), 14.

[14]Mark Christiansen, "Tripling Writing and Omitting Readings in Freshman English: An Experiment," *College Composition and Communication,* Vol. 16 (May, 1965), 123-124.

[15]Paul B. Diederich, *Measuring Growth in English.* Urbana: Ill.: National Council of Teachers of English, 1974, p. 22.

[16]Braddock and others, *Research in Written Composition,* pp. 69-70.

- *Correcting.* Praising what students do well improves their writing more than correction of what they do badly.[17] [18] Intensive correction does no more to improve writing than moderate correction.
- *Reading.* Writing programs that encourage students to read extensively and that devote time to the study of written prose are effective in improving student writing.[19] [20] [21] [22] [23]
- *Prewriting.* Most recently, researchers have been focusing more on the process of writing itself and less on teacher behavior and writing as a finished product. These researchers have found that an emphasis on prewriting activities leads to improved student writing. *Prewriting,* in this instance, means any exercise, experience, or activity intended to encourage a writer's creative thought prior to the act of drafting his or her manuscript. These structured motivational activities may occur before or during the writing process and involve students in thinking,

talking, writing, and working in groups. (See page 11 in the handbook for a further discussion of prewriting.)[24] [25] [26] [27] [28]

- *Modeling.* Sharing writing with peers, editing in groups, imitating prose models, and encouraging teacher participation in writing assignments are all practices that have resulted in the improvement of student writing.[29] [30]

More and more writing programs based on the research findings cited above are beginning to emerge. Preeminent among these programs are the University of California, Berkeley/Bay Area Writing Project

Praising what students do well improves their writing more than correction of what they do badly.

[17]Daniel J. Dieterich, "Composition Evaluation: Options and Advice," *English Journal,* Vol. 61 (November, 1972), 1,269.

[18]Charles R. Cooper, "Research Roundup: Oral and Written Composition," *English Journal,* Vol. 63 (September, 1974), 103.

[19]Strom, *Research in Grammar and Usage,* pp. 6-7.

[20]*Encyclopedia of Educational Research,* Fourth Edition. Edited by Robert L. Ebel. London: The Macmillan Company, Collier-Macmillan Limited, 1969, p. 450.

[21]Heys, "The Theme-a-Week Assumption," p. 322.

[22]Christiansen, "Tripling Writing and Omitting Readings in Freshman English," p. 124.

[23]Nathan S. Blount, "Research on Teaching Literature, Language and Composition," in *Second Handbook of Research on Teaching.* Edited by Robert M. W. Travers. Chicago: Rand McNally and Co., 1973, p. 1,084.

[24]Charles R. Cooper, "Research Roundup: Oral and Written Composition," *English Journal,* Vol. 63 (September, 1974), 102.

[25]Charles R. Cooper, "Research Roundup: Oral and Written Composition," *English Journal,* Vol. 62 (November, 1973), 1,202.

[26]Lee Odell, "Measuring the Effect of Instruction in Pre-Writing," *Research in the Teaching of English,* Vol. 8 (fall, 1974), 240.

[27]Janet Emig, *The Composing Processes of Twelfth Graders.* Urbana, Ill.: National Council of Teachers of English, 1971, pp. 98-99.

[28]Charles K. Stallard, "An Analysis of the Writing Behavior of Good Student Writers," *Research in the Teaching of English,* Vol. 8 (fall, 1974), 211, 217.

[29]Charles R. Cooper, "Research Roundup: Oral and Written Composition," *English Journal,* Vol. 64 (December, 1975), 74.

[30]Doris V. Gunderson, "Research in the Teaching of English," *English Journal,* Vol. 60 (September, 1971), 793.

The language arts are interrelated and are more difficult to learn when they are taught in isolation from each other.

and an outgrowth from it, the California Writing Project, which includes 19 writing centers across the state. These centers provide teachers of writing with in-service education, which reflects the findings of the current research in writing. (See Appendix B for a description of the California Writing Project and a list of the projects.)

(NOTE: For additional information on research in the teaching of writing, see the entries in Selected References; also see "We Are All Out-of-Date Scientists," by Owen Thomas, in *Practical Ideas for Teaching Writing as a Process.*)

Integration of the Language Arts

The language arts—listening, speaking, reading, and writing—are interrelated and are more difficult to learn when they are taught in isolation from each other. People learn language in a sequence that moves from listening and speaking to reading and writing; therefore, an effective writing program necessarily builds on and is reinforced by oral language experiences and is enhanced by extensive reading.

Similarly, the conventions of language—such as spelling, grammar, punctuation, diction, and usage—are not learned well when taught in isolation. They are best learned at appropriate points in the writing process, because students can practice the interrelationships of the skills in their own writing. The immediacy of the effort helps to make the conventions more understandable and meaningful for them.

Students may also perceive the relationships of the writing process

to the development of cognitive skills and imagination. As they receive new information through reading and listening, they can begin to integrate that information into their framework of past knowledge by speaking and writing about it. Because the writing process evokes thought and imagination, writing can be an effective tool for learning in all subjects.

(NOTE: For further reading on integration of the language arts, see the entries for Michael Marland, Nancy Martin, and James Moffett in the Selected References.)

Motivation for Students to Write

At the heart of the writing process is motivation, and teachers can do much to help their students become motivated to write. Students want to express themselves and communicate with others, but they often believe that what they have to say is unimportant and, as a result, they tend to be careless in their writing. They will believe that their writing is important if they have experiences that confirm that belief. Such experiences are likely to occur if they are given opportunities to write on topics of deep concern to them or with which they are intimately familiar.

When writers are in control of their topics, they experience the power of language. Students know that they can anger, delight, and comfort others with oral language, but they seldom experience such reactions to their writing. However, they realize how powerful written language can be when they receive responses to their writing. For example, if, through their writing, students receive a pamphlet in the mail or bring about a change in school rules, they begin to realize that writing can be useful and powerful and that how something is written is important.

Students must also have confidence that they are capable of expressing themselves on paper. "Writer's block," the fear of writing, often occurs because of the students' overriding concern with correctness, not because they have nothing to say about a topic. This paralyzing concern is learned behavior that can be reversed by teachers who reinforce everything their students do right. The confidence students gain through such affirmation will help them achieve correctness and facility with written expression.

Finally, students need to believe that writing is valuable. Most students seldom see adults writing. Indeed, writing is a private act, often done in isolation. As a result, students seldom witness the stages of pondering, revising, and editing that occur in the writing process. The more that students witness teachers and parents writing, the more likely they are to place value on writing. When teachers and parents do writing assignments with students and share their successes and failures, the students are more likely to develop an appreciation of the value of writing.

Unless students perceive the art of writing as important, valuable, and possible, they tend to produce merely isolated samples of writing that are relatively lifeless, perfunctory, awkward, and dull. When their teachers and parents dwell on correctness rather than on content, students are likely to see writing only as an obligation imposed from without rather than as a need to express oneself. (See Appendix A for the National Council of Teachers of English's suggestions

"*Achilles exists only through Homer. Take away the art of writing from this world, and you will probably take away its glory.*"

François René de Chateaubriand

for parents on "How to Help Your Child Become a Better Writer.")

(NOTE: For further reading on motivating students to write, see the entries for Peter Elbow and Ken Macrorie in the Selected References.)

The Use of Computers in Writing

Recognizing that motivation is "at the heart of the writing process," an increasing number of teachers throughout the nation are experimenting with microcomputers to motivate children to improve their writing skills, especially in the revising and editing stages of the writing process. Although it may be too early to determine how much long-term impact these machines will have in helping students express themselves in writing, the excitement of those who are using computers to teach writing is unmistakable. (For a further discussion of the use of computers, see Stephen Marcus's article, "Computers in the Curriculum," in Appendix C.)

The consensus of those who have used computers to teach writing indicates that such machines offer these advantages:

- They permit students to record ideas much faster than they could record them with a pencil and paper; thus, fluency is increased.
- They make revising and editing much easier, thus facilitating sentence combining and the process of reexamining and refining what has been written.
- With most word processors, students can produce more legible copies of what they have "written" than they can with paper and pen.
- Material can be stored more easily.
- They make the writing task easier for handicapped students.
- Through certain types of programming, students can have their work evaluated quickly and objectively for very specific matters, such as spelling.

Although the reports from those who have used word processors to

teach writing are, for the most part, very positive, many of them offer these cautions:

- Prior to purchasing equipment and software, educators should determine their students' precise needs, and they should do appropriate reading and research regarding what is available in this rapidly growing field. (Educators may find the Department of Education's *Educational Software Preview Guide* particularly helpful in selecting appropriate software for their educational programs.)

- Those who purchase computers for classroom use should make certain that the equipment and its accompanying software have word processing capabilities. Computers that do not include word processors are of little value in programs for the teaching of writing.

- Teachers must be fully trained not only in the operation of the equipment but also in its applications to the writing process.

- Schools should not try to implement a program with too few computers to meet the needs of their students.

- An expert who can correct any malfunctions of the equipment must be immediately available.

- Some students will write better with paper and pencil than with a computer.

- Students who do not know how to type need to be given some instruction at the keyboard before they use the word processor.

(NOTE: For additional information on the use of computers in writing, see

Appendix C and the entries in the Selected References for Hugh Burns, Robert Levin and Claire Doyle, Peter McWilliams, Helen Schwartz, William Wresch, and William Zinsser; also see *Computers in Composition Instruction, Teaching Writing Through Technology,* and the Department of Education's *Computers in Education: Goals and Content* and the *Technology in the Curriculum* series.

The Use of This Handbook

This handbook is not intended to be prescriptive; it is intended to be a source of motivation and guidance for those at the school site level who wish to examine and perhaps change a school's writing program. Neither is it intended to be exhaustive in its recommendations and examples regarding the establishment of writing programs. Rather, it is intended to prompt curriculum planners at the school site level to inform themselves regarding what is known about the teaching and learning of writing and then to plan

This handbook is not intended to be prescriptive; it is intended to be a source of motivation and guidance for those at the school site level who wish to examine and perhaps change a school's writing program.

and implement a new writing program, as appropriate.

Accordingly, the checklist near the end of this document should be thought of as a means for assessing teaching materials, methodologies, approaches, and curriculum guides, not as a means for evaluating teachers. It is the writing program which must be scrutinized. This will require classroom observations; interviews of students, teachers, administrators, and parents; a study of the learning environment in the school; a review of pertinent curriculum guides; an examination of student writing; and a study of the teaching materials and text-books currently in use.

II. The Writing Process

The writing process might be described as having several stages or phases, including prewriting, writing, responding, revising, editing, developing skills with the conventions of writing, evaluating, and postwriting. While the writing program should include opportunities for students to become aware of these stages and to have learning experiences in each of them, the stages should not be thought of as necessarily sequential or linear in nature. Rather, the stages are largely recursive; for example, during the writing stage students might edit for the conventions of writing (spelling, punctuation, grammar, usage) as they proceed with composing their ideas. Similarly, many will revise as they go and then revise again later after they receive responses to what they have written.

Some writing assignments may not require attention to each of the stages identified above. Informal writing in journals and brief written exercises to help students attain greater fluency, for example, may not require as much attention to each of the stages as essay writing or other formal expository writing may require. Also, the amount of attention that should be given to each stage will vary from student to student. However, because several of these stages are frequently overlooked in writing programs,

conscious efforts should be made to provide students with experiences with all of them. In any event, it is important to keep in mind that experienced writers generate ideas before they write and that they change their ideas and generate new ones as they write. Accordingly, a major goal of a writing program is to acquaint students with the stages that experienced writers go through as they compose and refine their writing and to help students experience those stages in their own writing.

Prewriting— the First Stage

Prewriting is the first stage in the writing process. It includes any experience, activity, or exercise that motivates a person to write, generates material and ideas for writing, or focuses a writer's attention on a particular subject. Prewriting stimulates and enlarges thought and moves writers from the stage of thinking about a writing task to the act of writing. This stage in the writing process is frequently overlooked, and students are merely expected to write without being motivated to do so.

For younger or less experienced students in particular, prewriting can be thought of as planned learning experiences that occur between the time they are aware of

The writing process has several stages or phases, including prewriting, writing, responding, revising, editing, developing skills with the conventions of writing, evaluating, and postwriting.

having to write and the time they begin to write. Later, as they become more experienced with writing, they may have less need for extensively planned prewriting experiences. They will begin to find their sources of motivation and ideas for writing in their daily environment or in their reading. However, many students have not yet reached this level of sophistication with the writing process. Carefully planned prewriting experiences will help them to get started by helping them to discover that they have something to say and that they want to say it.

SUGGESTED PREWRITING ACTIVITIES

Those who plan writing programs should be resourceful in their efforts to develop and implement successful prewriting activities. Among them might be the following:

1. Provide an environment conducive to prewriting activities, with adequate materials to stimulate writing activities; e.g., works of literature, magazines, posters, photographs, word games, puppets, and so forth.
2. Provide motivation for writing; e.g., displaying student work, sharing written work with other classes, holding a language arts show, and so forth.
3. Make use of a significant piece of literature as a source of discussion leading to further research and, ultimately, writing.
4. Provide time for the class to discuss the writing assignments.

5. Provide a variety of activities for gathering information; e.g., viewing films; interviewing visitors, family, friends, and school personnel; taking opinion surveys—family, friends, and school personnel; hearing stories; reading self-selected materials; and going on field trips to interesting places in the community.
6. Provide opportunities for students to interact and to discuss informally with one another their ideas and plans as they begin to write.
7. Make use of the technique of "clustering" as a means for eliciting student writing. Using this technique, the teacher writes a key word on the chalkboard and then surrounds it with other associated words that are suggested by a group of students. By drawing lines to show relationships between the words in the cluster, the students begin to develop ideas and are ready to begin writing. Further information regarding this technique may be found in *Balancing the Hemispheres: Brain Research and the Teaching of Writing* by Mary Frances Claggett and Gabriele Lusser Rico.
8. Make use of improvisational drama and other dramatic activities, both within and outside the classrooms, as motivation for writing.
9. Lead the class in a brainstorming session on an announced topic during which all student contributions are listed. Students can then select

"It is one of the truths of life that, if you want to influence others, it is not enough to know a subject; you must also be able to express what you know."

H. G. Rickover

from among these and arrive at a more specific topic about which they will write.

(NOTE: For further information on prewriting, see the entries in the Selected References for Mary Frances Claggett and Gabriele Lusser Rico and for James Moffett; also see the chapters on prewriting and clustering in *Practical Ideas for Teaching Writing as a Process.*)

Writing—One Stage in the Process

Writing involves teachable skills, but a writing program that includes only skill development will ultimately prove ineffective. Attention must also be given to the composing process itself. Furthermore, most classroom writing should be seen as simply one stage in the entire process of producing a finished written statement. The process should begin with a series of carefully planned prewriting activities; after a first draft has been completed, the subsequent stages include receiving responses from the teacher, peers, and others; revising; editing; and learning to observe the conventions of language. Subsequent stages include evaluation and postwriting. The writing stage may require the least amount of time in the process.

For some writers who have spent sufficient time in the prewriting stage, the actual writing of the first draft will proceed smoothly and rapidly, often being completed in one sitting. At other times the same writer may struggle back and forth between prewriting, writing, and rewriting. However, the writing of the first draft can be thought of as the fulcrum of the writing process.

Writing, when it is not the mere transcribing or paraphrasing of someone else's work, is the written expression of the writer's ideas synthesized from experience. Writing is the revision of one's thinking that is narrowed to include only the subject at hand. A learning sequence based on this concept of writing might have students begin the process by watching someone else write one word or a simple sentence based on his or her personal experience. Then they would gradually take over the writing process themselves; and, finally, they would share the products with a specific audience. Later, as the students' abilities to engage in abstract thinking increase, the students can use their abilities to communicate through writing as a means of taking in, processing, and communicating new information and ideas.

An effective writing program at any level provides many opportunities for students to develop confidence and fluency, free of the sometimes paralyzing fear of making errors in their writing. Those in charge of the writing program will recognize that only after students have developed this freedom and confidence will they be able to consider adequately the needs of their audience and the purpose of their writing.

In addition to developing confidence and fluency in their writing, students should have experiences with many types of writing. Too often, they are asked to express themselves in only two or three

"The writer must therefore constantly ask himself: What am I trying to say? Surprisingly often, he doesn't know."
William Zinsser

13

modes of discourse or domains of writing. There are a great many types of writing in both presentational and discursive modes, and the intellectual growth of students is dependent, in large measure, on the breadth and depth of their experiences with them. Furthermore, because of the centralities of literature in the English language arts curriculum, response to literature should be a prime subject of student writing. (For more information about these issues, see James Moffett's *Teaching the Universe of Discourse.*)

Writing to Develop Fluency

Fluency is the facility writers have for using appropriate language and putting their thoughts on paper. If writers are fluent, their words flow onto the page with relative ease. Students who write fluently are likely to discover that they have much to say. They express their ideas, feelings, and reactions to events around them relatively easily. They are not preoccupied with matters of correctness in their first draft.

Students lacking fluency are easy to identify. They fidget. They are easily distracted. They do not know what to write about and usually need to have the directions for a writing assignment explained several times. They need constant assurance that their work is acceptable. They often are so preoccupied with correctness that they write very little. Writing for them is a word-by-word struggle.

Teachers can improve their students' abilities to write fluently by motivating them to write daily and extensively and in more than one subject area. For example, they could be asked to write entries in a journal or diary, letters, vignettes, reports, brief narrations and descriptions, and précis. Having students write as many words as

"True ease in writing comes from art, not chance,
As those move easiest who have learned to dance."

Alexander Pope

possible within a specific time without worrying about correctness is also an excellent way to help them increase their fluency. As students develop fluency in their writing, they can begin to concern themselves with observing language conventions and with addressing specific purposes and audiences.

SUGGESTED ACTIVITIES TO HELP STUDENTS DEVELOP FLUENCY

1. Write as much as they can about a given subject within a specified period of time without the pressure of competing or of being graded.
2. Keep journals or learning logs about their classroom experiences. A learning log is a student-maintained log in which the student, through writing, attempts to explain a presentation, concept, or lesson just learned. This explanation may be directed to the teacher, the writer, a close friend, an imaginary audience, or others.
3. Listen to stories and then record their thoughts about what they have heard.
4. Keep notes, journals, logs, or diaries of school experiences, such as readings, discussions, experiments, projects, and excursions. These can later be used for "writing for an audience."
5. Dictate ideas, stories, or descriptions of events to another person who records the material. This can be an easy way of producing a first draft, which the students can revise.
6. Participate in clustering activities at appropriate times. (See page 12 for an explanation of this technique.)
7. Make lists of familiar objects.
8. Read extensively and analytically the works of fluent writers.

Writing for an Audience

Writers may address numerous audiences, but they are their own first audience. Writing for oneself can take various forms, such as journals, diaries, learning logs, and poems. Such egocentric writing may not be fully understandable to others. However, such writing is most important in helping writers discover what they believe, know, and wish to say before they write for a larger audience.

Among the other audiences to whom students may wish to write are parents, other family members, classmates, friends, neighbors, and pen pals. The classroom climate

should be such that they feel they can write to their teachers as trusted adults, as partners in learning, and, only later, as evaluators. These known audiences require that writers communicate their feelings and ideas in forms more controlled than those they use when writing only for themselves. As they write, they must constantly envision their audience. To their friends, teachers, and parents, they may wish to write letters, brief narrations, poems, vignettes, plays, reports, research papers, and brief autobiographies. To more distant readers, they may wish to write business letters, letters of request, letters to editors, news reports, articles, and instructions.

Ultimately, students should learn to write to broader unknown audiences. Here again, they should try to envision the characteristics of the broader audience they are addressing. As they do so, they will need to adjust the nature of their diction and rhetoric with this larger audience in mind.

SUGGESTED ACTIVITIES TO HELP STUDENTS IMPROVE THEIR ABILITIES TO WRITE FOR VARIOUS AUDIENCES

1. Select a real or imagined event (news report, sporting event, accident), and write about the event twice, each time to a different audience.

2. Write to persuade a particular person or group to agree to do something unusual.

3. Write letters to a given audience for a specific purpose (get well, complaint, letter to an editor).

4. Write about what they have learned in various subjects for audiences composed of younger students or students who are unfamiliar with the subject.

5. Interview people in the school or community, and prepare a written report of the interview for publication for a general audience.

6. Write the same message in several different forms to several different audiences.

7. Write parts of stories by creating new endings, different points of view, new characters, or additional incidents.

8. Select an audience for descriptions, vignettes, short narrations, stories, or poems; use story starters, photographs, magazine pictures, art, music, or their own journal entries as sources of motivation.

9. React to books they have read in these ways:
    a. Select a character and write a story that places him or

"Every piece of writing is shaped not only by its function (or use), but also by a conception of the audience to whom it is addressed."

Arthur N. Applebee

her in a totally different setting.

b. Write a letter to one of the characters.

c. Have a character write a letter to the editor or a columnist.

d. Write a report of an interview or conversation with one of the characters.

Writing with Purpose

In addition to learning to write fluently and to address a variety of audiences, students also need to identify a specific purpose for each piece of writing. Indeed, the purpose can be a prime source of motivation for writing. Examples of possible purposes might include writing to inform, to explain, to comfort, to record, to persuade, to complain, or to entertain. Purpose should be determined early in the writing process so that it can serve as an underlying guide to the diction and rhetoric used. Purpose will often determine the mode of discourse the writer may choose. Monologue, narrative, exposition, and argumentation are determined by the writer's purpose, and students should have experience in writing in various modes. (See James Moffett's *Active Voice*.)

Having a purpose is also important when decisions about grammar and usage must be made, especially during the revision and editing stages of the process. Students need to have experiences in writing for a wide range of purposes so that they may learn what effect different purposes can have on the writing process. They need to become aware of semantics or the emotional overtones of many words and to use these advisedly.

Deciding on the purpose of a piece of writing is related to decisions regarding the nature of the audience, and students need practice in discovering this interrelationship. A useful method is to have them write to different audiences with a single purpose in mind or to have them write to the same audience for varied purposes.

Students may require help in defining various purposes for writing, and teachers should help them discover the writers' purposes in the various selections they read; e.g., writing that informs, evokes, explores, or persuades. Finally, students should be introduced to these purposes for writing as the need for them arises, rather than according to a fixed outline.

SUGGESTED ACTIVITIES TO HELP STUDENTS IMPROVE THEIR ABILITIES TO WRITE FOR A PURPOSE

1. Compile lists of purposes for writing; e.g., to inform, to explain, to delight, to persuade.
2. Study and discuss models of various purposes for writing.
3. Identify the writers' purposes in what is read.
4. Write on the same topic with different purposes in mind.
5. Rewrite a completed piece for a new purpose.
6. Parody a piece of writing to show shift in purpose.

(NOTE: For additional information on writing, see the entries for the following authors in the Selected References: Ann Berthoff, James Britton, Roger Garrison, Jack Hailey, James Moffett and Betty Wagner, Donald Murray, and Mina Shaughnessy; also see *Practical Ideas for Teaching Writing as a Process*.)

Responding—Reacting to What Was Written

Through a reader's response, which can occur at almost any time in the writing process, a writer makes overt contact with an audience. The reaction of a reader to a piece of writing is usually expressed through questions, suggestions, and statements to the writer about the content or form of what was written. The audience can be a teacher, a peer, a group, a holistic scoring team, or anyone who responds to a piece of writing. It should be borne in mind, however, that response is not the same as evaluation, because it is usually a quick first reaction that is general in nature.

One effective way of providing student writers with useful audience responses is by having groups of peers provide the student writers with reactions to early drafts of their writing. These comments serve to help writers clarify their ideas and purposes and to eliminate mechanical errors which block reader comprehension. As students make suggestions about the writing of others, they gain a better understanding of the writing process themselves. Since good student writers rely heavily on revision as a means of clarifying and improving their writing, audience response to their writing is particularly valuable in the revision process.

SUGGESTED ACTIVITIES WHICH ELICIT RESPONSES TO WRITING

To help students respond constructively to each other's work, teachers:

1. May conduct whole-class response sessions by using reproduced copies of the students' work or by making use of an overhead projector to examine the work. To avoid embarrassing students and possibly discouraging them from writing, the identification of each student writer can be concealed in such sessions. Teachers may role play different types of responses to teach students how to make specific observations which go beyond initial vague and general statements of likes and dislikes.

2. Might provide response sheets, forms, or open-ended sentences that allow students to make written responses to each other's writing. Response sheets may call for responses by individuals, or they may contain space for several people to respond.

3. Might provide demonstrations of the group processes involved in conducting effective sessions on responding to student writing.

4. Might give students two versions of the same piece of writing, and ask them to comment on the differences.

5. Might arrange small response groups of two to five students. Encourage students to share their work by reading aloud or by exchanging papers. In this way, all members of the group will receive immediate audience reaction while they are in the process of composing.

6. Might establish a schedule of individual consultations with students regarding their writing.

7. Might employ the "Read-Around Group" procedure as a means of providing extensive and immediate responses to student writing without increasing the teachers' workload.

(NOTE: For additional information on responding, as a stage in the writing process, see the entries for Peter Elbow and Mary K. Healy in the Selected References. For specific information on the read-around group technique, see Jenee Gossard's description in *Practical Ideas for Teaching Writing as a Process*.)

Through a reader's response, which can occur at almost any time in the writing process, a writer makes overt contact with an audience.

Revising—Reexamining What Was Written

The response process is an essential step in helping students see their work through the eyes of others. Revision is the next step.

For many teachers and students, the word *revise* means "proofread, edit, and copy it over in ink." A true revision, however, involves a process during which a writer "resees" and "rethinks" a piece of his or her writing many times while writing and rereading it, with special emphasis on how effectively the written material communicates his or her intent to the audience.

During this recursive or recurring process, students need to consider such matters as unity, development, order, clarity, emphasis, and word choice. They also need to examine their work in terms of its organization and the possible need for reasons, examples, or other supporting evidence. They might consider adding further supporting information, qualifying details, concrete examples, sensory details, and transitional words, phrases, and sentences. They might need to change the emphasis or focus of a statement or to insert arguments to meet possible objections to what they have said. They might try reading their work aloud to try to discover possible misstatements, errors, or sources of confusion. They might try rereading their work to see if such matters as the how, where, what, and when of their statements have been adequately addressed. The degree to which they attend to all of these matters will, of course, depend on the skill and maturity of the students. In any event, revision is a recursive process taking place during writing, rewriting, reading, and rereading.

A well-planned writing program provides instruction in the techniques of revision and opportunities for students to receive responses prior to revising what they have written. It is important to remember, however, that not all writing needs to be taken through the revision stage. Part of learning to revise is learning to decide which pieces of writing deserve or are ready for revision.

Much student writing, as mentioned earlier, should be done for the purpose of developing fluency or for reinforcing the learning of subject matter. The value of such writing is in having the student do it, not in producing a finished piece of writing. Therefore, it does not need to be carefully evaluated and revised, but the teacher may wish to give students credit for doing the writing exercises. However, it is important that students at all levels be taught that revision is an essential step in producing a piece of writing for an audience, and they should be given frequent opportunities to take pieces of writing through the revision stage.

SUGGESTED ACTIVITIES TO ENCOURAGE STUDENTS TO REVISE THEIR WRITING

1. Distribute copies of writing by peers or from published sources, and have students analyze the passages, raising as many questions as they can regarding clarity, meaning, and emphasis.
2. Have students in pairs exchange their papers and indicate to each other where clarification or more information is needed.
3. As a daily writing exercise, give students a general declarative sentence and ask them to turn it into a vivid paragraph by making use of concrete and sensory details.
4. Have each student write about a topic for several different

Revision involves a process during which a writer "resees" and "rethinks" a piece of his or her writing many times while writing and rereading it.

audiences. For example, a student might write about personal experiences for parents, a close friend, a sibling, a boss, or for the school newspaper.

5. Have students choose one paragraph or section of a paper, or one paper out of several similar papers, to revise carefully prior to its evaluation.
6. Give students examples of the revisions professional writers have made of their own writing.

(NOTE: For additional information on revising as a stage in the writing process, see the entries for Richard Lanham and for Iris and Sidney Tiedt in the Selected References; also see *Practical Ideas for Teaching Writing as a Process*.)

Editing—Refining What Was Written

Editing, which is the refinement stage of the writing process, is the cleaning up and correcting of a piece of writing. Although a certain amount of editing may be done throughout the writing process, the major work occurs prior to the evaluating and post-writing stages. A variety of people may assist the student writer with the editing process, including peers, teachers, tutors, aides, and parents.

Editing may be divided into the following categories, which identify matters requiring attention during this refinement step of the writing process: (1) the conventions of writing (grammar, usage, capitalization, punctuation, spelling, paragraphing, and syllabication); (2) diction, that is, examining a piece of writing for appropriate, effective, and precise word choices; (3) syntax, which includes adding transitions, changing sentence structure, and correcting awkward constructions; (4) accuracy of text, which includes the checking of quotations, dates, footnotes, and tabular data; (5) proper manuscript form (margins, headings, subheads, paging); and (6) proofreading and reading the work to ensure that what is on the page is what the writer intended to say.

Just as authors edit their writing prior to submitting it to a publisher, so student writers need to edit their work prior to submitting it for evaluation. They need to learn how editing adds to the clarity, correctness, and presentation of a paper. An effective writing program acknowledges the importance of editing, helps students learn to appreciate the value of editing, and provides practice for writers to learn to edit their work.

SUGGESTED ACTIVITIES TO TEACH EDITING SKILLS TO STUDENTS

1. Provide students with written standards for editing, such as a format sheet, proofreading symbols, an editing checklist, and a stylebook. (A number of stylebooks are available, but two of the most complete are *The Chicago Manual of Style* and *The McGraw-Hill Style Manual*.)
2. Help students develop, then use, an editing checklist as they edit their own or other students' papers.
3. Lead an editing session. Teachers may find *The Chicago Manual of Style, The McGraw-Hill Style Manual*, and other stylebooks helpful in carrying out this task.
4. Dictate statements for students to write and punctuate.
5. Have students do sentence-combining exercises. (Teachers may find Frank O'Hare's book, *Sentence Combining: Improving Student Writing*

"Many of the professional people and educators who complain most loudly about poor student writing are saved by their wives, their scholarly friends, their editors, and their secretaries, who adeptly convert incoherent writing into acceptable prose."

H. Mark Johnson

Without Formal Grammar Instruction, helpful in carrying out this exercise.)

6. Have students work in pairs or small groups to edit each other's work.
7. Have students edit examples of writing that contain the specific types of problems that are usually corrected during the editing process.

Developing Skill with the Conventions of Writing

Students can best develop their skill with the conventions of writing as the need for it arises in their work, rather than according to a fixed program. Writing itself, then, becomes the basis for determining which skills need to be learned by which students and at which time. Some writing skills, such as those needed for writing technical papers or preparing advertising copy, may never be developed by some students, because the need for learning them may never arise. Other skills, however, such as building one's vocabulary and using correct spelling, punctuation, usage, and grammatical constructions, are needed by all students in order to ensure that they write clearly and correctly.

One key to successful instruction in the conventions of writing is to work as much as possible with the language which students produce themselves. Confronting them with their own written expression in the light of the conventions or rules of the language often produces the most lasting learning. The issue of subject-verb agreement, for example, becomes important when students see how the lack of such agreement can create confusion in their own writing. Students should be encouraged to edit their own writing by listening to the flow of their language. Gross errors often become obvious when written material is read aloud. Although objective tests can reveal much about the students' knowledge of language conventions, the degree of their mastery of these conventions is best revealed in their own writing.

Various skills are best learned at particular stages of the writing process. For example, vocabulary is often expanded during prewriting activities, such as brainstorming and clustering. Decisions about usage and grammar often occur during the revision stage when writers may rearrange or combine their sentences. Typically, spelling and punctuation become important when writers proofread their papers in the editing stage of the writing process.

Since students learn at different rates and in different ways, the art of teaching writing conventions is to know when a student is ready to deal with each skill. Learning grammatical analysis, usage, and other conventions makes little sense to students until they are writing, grappling with choices, and making decisions. For example, it is futile to teach the uses of the semicolon unless the student has grasped the concept of coordinate elements. Need appears to be the best motivator for developing writing skills, and it is during the writing process itself when students experience the greatest need for knowing how to use the conventions of writing. Teachers should capitalize on this and be pre-

pared to help their students with such matters at that time.

SUGGESTED ACTIVITIES TO HELP STUDENTS DEVELOP SKILL WITH THE CONVENTIONS OF WRITING

1. Diagnose students' writing skills through analytical scoring, noting everything that was done well.
2. Have lists of correct examples of specific writing skills to hand to students who have not demonstrated competency in specific skill areas.
3. Develop prewriting activities that generate vocabulary.
4. Provide spelling and punctuation checklists for students during the editing stage.
5. Categorize errors in writing so that students notice repeated errors in each category.
6. Provide practice with sentence-combining activities to illustrate sentence construction, variety, and ways of achieving economy of expression.
7. Demonstrate how changes in audience and purpose affect decisions about diction, grammar, and usage.
8. Help students make effective use of grammar and usage handbooks. (Although a large number of books on grammar and usage are available, some of the most widely used and respected books are *American Usage and Style: The Consensus* by Roy H. Copperud; *Elements of Style* by William Strunk and E. B. White; *Modern American Usage* by Wilson Follett, edited by Jacques Barzun; and *Writer's Guide and Index to English* by Wilma and David Ebbitt. Other very

useful references are cited in the Selected References.)

(NOTE: For additional information on the conventions of writing, see the entries in the Selected References for Frank O'Hare and Gail Siegel; and see *Practical Ideas for Teaching Writing as a Process.*)

Evaluating— Judging the Writing Constructively

Evaluation is only one aspect of the postwriting stage of the writing process; thus, it should be kept in perspective. Commonly, teachers have "taught" composition primarily by emphasizing evaluation. Students wrote; teachers corrected. Over-emphasis on this one part of the writing process should be avoided, because it could teach students that correctness rather than the communication of meaning is what writing is all about. Evaluation should be simply one stage in the overall process.

It is vital to the development of student writing that evaluation be used to support, not thwart, students in their work. In order for evaluation to promote growth, writers must know in advance the purpose of the evaluation, the criteria by which the work will be judged, and who the evaluator(s) will be. The purposes for which the evaluation is conducted may range from determining the specific needs of each student to assessing a school's curriculum. Whatever the reason for evaluation, the purpose should determine the methods of evaluation. Awareness of this guideline will help evaluators avoid excessive and inappropriate testing

"The great poet, in writing himself, writes his time."
T. S. Eliot

Evaluation is only one aspect of the postwriting stage of the writing process; thus, it should be kept in perspective.

and help them to make more effective use of test data.

Objective tests of the conventions of language can serve a useful function. They can reveal to some extent a student's knowledge of the mechanics of language in such areas as spelling, punctuation, correct usage, grammatical analysis, and vocabulary. Indeed, there is evidence to indicate that the data from objective tests intended to measure the knowledge of language mechanics of a given group of students will correlate well with data produced from writing samples of the same group.[1] Such data are also useful for diagnostic purposes.

Data from objective tests, however, are more valuable as indicators of the editing than the composing skills of students. They tend to reveal more about students' abilities to detect errors in the writing of others than about the students' abilities to compose on their own. For example, such tests may reveal that certain students can differentiate between sentences and sentence fragments, but they may not reveal much about the abilities of the students to compose sentences.

This is not to say, however, that the storehouse of information accumulated during recent years under the California Assessment Program (CAP) should be overlooked by those who examine a school's writing program. Objective test data produced under this program are readily available and can reveal a great deal about the writing programs of the schools in California. (See the latest annual report of *Student Achievement in California Schools.*)

---

[1]*An Assessment of the Writing Performance of California High School Seniors.* Sacramento: California State Department of Education, 1977.

Furthermore, significant efforts have been made under the California Assessment Program to develop and use test items that are based on the content and recommendations regarding written language skills in the *English–Language Arts Framework for California Public Schools.* Indeed, the revised sixth grade CAP test and the new eighth grade test include items which require students to identify strengths and weaknesses in actual samples of student writing. The items should make the new tests very useful for diagnostic purposes and should make them much more than merely traditional multiple-choice tests of a student's editing skills. In addition, the program also accumulates data at school site levels regarding the frequency of writing assignments, student attitudes toward writing, and student performance. Such information should be very useful to curriculum planners at the school site level.

Securing and scoring samples of student writing should be central in efforts to evaluate writing, whether it is done on an individual or a group basis. And it should be remembered that the scoring of writing samples will vary with the purpose of the evaluation; for example:

- An analytic scale is a list of the prominent features or characteristics of a piece of writing. In the best analytic scoring guides, the features selected for evaluation arise out of the rhetorical context of the writing assignment—that is, from the purpose and audience designated in the rhetorical situation. The least defensible analytic guides are those in which universal features of writing are established without regard to the rhetorical context or the meaning of the writing assignment or the mode of discourse.

• Holistic evaluation of writing is a guided procedure for sorting or ranking written pieces. The rater takes a piece of writing and either (1) matches it with another piece in a graded series of pieces; (2) scores it for the prominence of certain features important to that kind of writing; or (3) assigns it a letter or number grade. The placing, scoring, or grading occurs quickly, impressionistically, after the rater has practiced the procedure with other raters. What is common to all forms of holistic evaluation is that the reader makes a quick, general impression of the paper by balancing simultaneously multiple features of the piece of writing. Holistic scoring guides range from those in which criteria are not clearly discernible to those in which criteria are clearly specified. The type of holistic scoring guide devised will depend on the purpose of the assessment.

• Primary trait scoring was developed for scoring the essays from the second (1974) writing assessment of the National Assessment of Educational Progress. Primary trait scoring guides focus the rater's attention on those features of a piece that are relevant to the kind of discourse it is—to the special blend of audience, speaker's role, purpose, and subject required by that kind of discourse and by the particular writing task. With this approach readers focus on the important thinking and text-making abilities demonstrated by the student and look past errors in grammatical correctness and mechanics. The latter

are usually tabulated separately through error counts or special analyses on a subset of the papers. Primary trait scoring is especially appropriate for assessing achievement in school because it makes the rater sensitive to the important learning that takes place as students develop the ability to handle many types of writing.

SUGGESTED ACTIVITIES TO ENHANCE THE EVALUATION OF STUDENTS' WRITING, BOTH COLLECTIVELY AND INDIVIDUALLY

1. Give students time and instructions on how to evaluate their own writing.
2. Have an entire class assess sample papers.
3. Give students training and experience in holistic scoring.
4. Help students develop a scoring guide for a given assignment.
5. Have students keep papers in individual folders for periodic review.
6. Announce the criteria for each assignment and the purposes of evaluation.
7. Provide appropriate staff development opportunities for all teachers of writing.

(NOTE: For additional information on evaluation, see the entries in the Selected References for Charles Cooper, Paul Diederich, Miles Myers, Lee Odell, and Edward M. White; also see *Practical Ideas for Teaching Writing as a Process.)*

Postwriting—Realizing the Importance of Writing

Postwriting includes all the activities that teachers and students can do with a finished piece of writing. They may chart it, illustrate it, post it, publish it, mail it, or discard it. This stage in the writing process is designed to help students

"It should be realized that there is no evidence that writing quality is the result of the accumulation by students of a series of subskills."

Edward M. White

realize the importance of, and establish value for, their own writing.

Too often students see their writing merely as products for teachers to grade. This limited view leads many students to compose stilted or meaningless prose rather than to communicate something that they care about to an audience they care about. By including postwriting activities as part of certain assignments, teachers can help their students realize the value of their writing.

Often, postwriting will involve the sharing of a written work with an audience. It may range from reading aloud to some form of publishing or display. At other times a piece of writing may be tucked away for personal use, discarded, or evaluated by district office personnel, teachers, students, or peers.

During the prewriting stage, an awareness of impending postwriting activities can motivate students and give them a sense of audience. Such activities can help them to realize that their work is appreciated and is useful.

SUGGESTED POSTWRITING ACTIVITIES

1. Publish student writing in class magazines, school magazines, classroom collections, and in community newspapers.
2. Have students share their writing by reading it aloud to a small group, a class, or a larger school or community audience.
3. Have students read their written scripts on local radio or cable television.
4. Have students adapt their narratives for dramatizing on radio or on the stage or for filming or videotaping.
5. Display in the school and community successful writing of students at all age and ability levels.
6. Have students exchange writing between classes and schools.
7. Have student response groups or editorial boards review student writing and edit it for publication.
8. Have students rewrite a piece by changing the mode, for example, from prose to poetry or drama, or from narration to exposition.
9. Have advanced bilingual students translate their work from one language to another.
10. Have students share writing about their cultural heritage with students of other cultural backgrounds.
11. Suggest that students use journals or other personal writing activities as a means of clarifying their values.
12. Have students use practical pieces of writing—job applications, resumes, letters, notes, advertising copy—in actual transactions with others.
13. Have students save their writing on topics of interest for later use as reference material for research work, family histories, or local archives.
14. Recognize superior writing through writing contests, awards, and assembly programs.
15. Permit students to set aside or even discard occasional pieces of writing which they do not wish to carry through to a finished product.

(NOTE: For additional information on postwriting, see the entries in the Selected References for Jerry Herman, James Moffett and Betty Wagner, and *Teaching the Universe of Discourse* by James Moffett.)

III. Implementing a Schoolwide Writing Program

General Considerations for a Schoolwide Program

To be effective, a writing program must be schoolwide in scope. Every teacher must be responsible for using writing as a means for learning in every subject area and at all age levels. Students will develop writing skills more effectively when writing is treated by all teachers as an integral part of the learning process rather than by a few teachers as a separate skill. Furthermore, it is not enough for teachers merely to expect students to write; the skills involved must be taught! Although some teachers may be better prepared to do this than others are, all should try to do more than merely ask students to write.

Writing is a valuable tool for helping students learn and retain information in all content areas. Experiences with various kinds of writing in each content area can increase the students' mastery of course content. In the process of ordering thoughts while writing, students arrive at a better understanding of the subject—a process of "coming to know"—than they would have without the writing experience. Expressed another way, through writing students can experience high levels of thinking, such as analysis, synthesis, appli-

cation, and evaluation. Writing, then, establishes a method through which students may express themselves, organize thoughts and information, communicate ideas and feelings, and demonstrate an understanding of the subject matter.

Serving many useful purposes, student writing provides valuable information for the teacher about the students' abilities, progress, interests, attitudes, insights, and values. When students write, they become involved in their own education and interested in what they are learning. If teachers establish a climate of trust and frequently allow students to write for a variety of purposes and audiences, they will help students develop self-confidence as well as their concepts of themselves as writers.

A written plan for a schoolwide writing program should be prepared and should become part of any other comprehensive schoolwide plan. By means of this written plan, all teachers in a school should understand their roles in helping to implement a schoolwide writing program. Furthermore, the written plan should help ensure schoolwide consistency regarding the teaching of writing.

Many children come to school with little experience with the written word. They have not engaged in some of the activities that many of us take for granted. They have not

"... writing can be a powerful process for discovering meaning rather than just transcribing an idea that is in some sense waiting fully developed in the writer's mind."

Arthur N. Applebee

watched adults read, have not been read to, have not helped make up shopping lists, or have not had their words written for them in a letter to their friends or grandparents. As a result, they are not aware that the printed word is a means of communication—nor, of course, have they absorbed, through experience, any of the skills involved in writing, as young children can so readily do if given the opportunity.

Children who have had few experiences with the written word need specific classroom activities to bridge the gap between their home experiences and (in some cases) home languages and what is expected of them at school. One cannot expect them to attempt to practice and master writing skills before they have had the experience of talking about something from their own life experiences and seeing that "talk" written for them. In other words, they need to have their words and simple sentences recorded for them. Failure to recognize this need and meet it with frequent, regular experiences of the type described leaves children unequipped with simple prerequisite skills. Such children are unable to make sense out of what they are asked to accomplish in school in both language arts and reading. (Teachers may find it helpful to secure from the National Council of Teachers of English copies of "How to Help Your Child Become a Better Writer," which has been reproduced in Appendix A of this handbook.)

(NOTE: For more information on implementing a schoolwide program, see the entries in the Selected References for Virginia Draper, Michael Marland, and Nancy Martin.)

"To deny language is finally to deny history, and that is what frightens me most about young people who can't write, particularly those who don't know it or don't care."

A. Bartlett Giamatti

SUGGESTED ACTIVITIES FOR A SCHOOL-WIDE WRITING PROGRAM

Some suggested classroom activities for implementing a school-wide writing program are outlined below. The lists are, of course, limited and readers are urged to add to them. The lists have been prepared under two main categories—those for beginners and those for students enrolled in specific subject areas:

- **Activities for Beginners**
1. To help students make the transition from communicating through speaking to communicating through writing, this sequence of activities might be followed:
   a. Have students talk about their experiences, including school-sponsored field trips.
   b. Elicit further oral responses with the help of pictures, drawings, interesting objects, and other similar stimuli.
   c. Record the students' responses, especially significant words or sentences.
   d. Have students illustrate what was written through art activities.
   e. Display the illustrations together with the recorded words and sentences.
   f. Help students, particularly those whose dominant language is other than English, learn the written symbol system of the English language, including the:
      (1) Alphabet
      (2) Formation of letters
      (3) Basic patterns of spelling
      (4) Basic conventions of the system in such areas as capitalization and punctuation

2. Dictation is a useful activity to help beginning students become aware of both the similarities and differences of the written and spoken language. Possible dictation exercises might include:

   a. Have students dictate group stories or poems for all to hear and enjoy. They might be based upon actual classroom experiences, including reactions to children's literature, creative dramatics, classroom visitors, animals in the classroom, and displays.

   b. Have students dictate individually to the teacher, classroom aide, community volunteer, or older students.

   c. Have students dictate short descriptive phrases for photographs, drawings, objects in the classroom, artwork, and science displays; put the phrases on labels for display purposes.

   d. Either in small groups or individually, have students dictate small books of stories, rhymes, or poems.

3. As students gain familiarity with the writing process by seeing their own thoughts written for them, encourage them to take over parts of the process themselves. In order to facilitate this, the teacher might:

   a. Have students trace over the letters of words in a simple sentence that they have dictated to someone who has written the sentence for them. They trace first with the index finger of the writing hand and later with a pen or pencil.

   b. Cut up a duplicate copy of the sentence into individual words, scramble them, and then ask the students to reconstruct the sentence, using the original as a model.

   c. Have the students copy the original sentence.

4. After students complete the sequence of activities outlined in the preceding item, they will, through this experience with words from their own vocabularies, be able to spell a few simple words. At this point, teachers can begin to make them aware that most words in English are spelled regularly but that some are spelled irregularly. Then they can be asked to write their own simple sentences, provided there are supportive materials in the room; e.g., word lists generated through brainstorming sessions, poems and songs that they can recite well enough to identify particular words, a phonics system with word lists associated with pictures, individual or class-generated dictionaries, and

A written plan for a schoolwide writing program should be prepared and should become part of any other comprehensive schoolwide plan.

so forth. Basic writing skills are acquired as students encounter the need for them in their writing.

5. Once students begin to compose their own sentences, they can be encouraged to begin writing for an audience. However, they should be provided the opportunity to incorporate other media, such as the fine arts, in this act of communication. Many young children will accomplish higher quality writing if they are allowed to produce in such media first and use this as the inspiration and guide for what they want to say.

- **Activities in Specific Subject Areas**

  1. Business Education
     a. To help students see the usefulness of writing, ask them to write and mail a variety of letters that will elicit responses.
     b. To increase student interest in business education, have them make plans for creating a business of their choice. Then have them write promotional material to advertise their new business or products.
     c. To help motivate students, allow them to type assignments for their other classes as partial fulfillment for course objectives in their typing class.

     d. To help students gain practical experience, ask them to write business letters and memos; fill out purchase orders, application forms, and invoices; and prepare budgets.

  2. English Language Arts
     a. To help students develop fluency and confidence and to encourage them to have a dialogue with their teacher, allow time for journal writing.
     b. To encourage having fun with language, have students retell an old tale or something read in class in their own words and in whatever mode they choose.
     c. To encourage students to become involved in their reading, have them pretend to be one of the characters in the book and ask them to write a letter to one of the other characters.
     d. To motivate students to write, frequently let them choose the topic so they can explore subjects of importance or interest to them.
     e. To build oral language skills, have students transcribe interviews.
     f. To lead in the development of a comprehensive writing program for students, English language arts teachers should make use of the many suggestions in Chapter II of this handbook.

  3. Social Studies
     a. To help students attain an appreciation for a significant historical event, have them write about it from the point of view of two or three different people who experienced it.
     b. To help students learn and retain information, have

them record in learning logs what they are studying, and permit them to refer to the logs during examinations.

c. To increase the students' understanding of the material being studied, have them answer study questions which require them to discuss cause and effect, to make comparisons, to draw conclusions, and to express their own evaluation of the material being studied.

d. To help students identify with the time and place they are studying, have them write appropriate songs, poems, letters to the editor, personal letters, and speeches; draw cartoons; or make up a newspaper.

e. Have students explore social studies concepts they do not understand by conducting the necessary research and then writing about their findings.

f. Have students write about an historical event as fiction.

4. Mathematics

a. To help students clarify a mathematics problem, have them write a step-by-step explanation of the solution.

b. To help students see the usefulness of mathematics concepts, have them solve a problem in a real-life situation. Have them state the problem and then write the solution.

c. To encourage students to feel comfortable using mathematical symbols, have them write a story or poem using mathematical symbols in place of some of the words. Encourage them to have fun with the language of mathematics.

d. To help students apply mathematics skills, have them write out word problems that fit given formulae.

5. Science

a. To encourage understanding and retention, frequently allow time for students to record in their own words what they have learned or what still confuses them. Read their learning logs periodically to clear up any inaccuracies and to praise well-written entries. If students can refer to these logs during examinations, they will be motivated to write clearly and concisely.

b. To help increase comprehension, encourage students to explain a new term or process more clearly than it was explained in the text. The best explanation could be posted or kept in a folder to help students who were absent.

c. To encourge students to think more about what they are studying, have them pretend to be a known scientist writing to a colleague or writing a letter to a newspaper in defense of an unpopular theory.

d. To help students learn to read science problems, ask them to write them. They

Students will develop writing skills more effectively when writing is treated by all teachers as an integral part of the learning process rather than by a few teachers as a separate skill.

might write questions and answers for possible use on the next examination.

6. Foreign Languages
   a. To give students the opportunity to use new vocabulary, plan language experience activities that help them develop oral language skills and use written language.
   b. To make students aware of the contributions the language they are studying has made to English, encourage the students to keep a list of English words that come from that language.
   c. To help students gain an appreciation of the culture of the people who speak the language they are learning, have them prepare notes describing a trip they would like to make to that country.
   d. To give students the opportunity to consider the advantages of being bilingual, have them write about the benefits of being able to write and speak in two languages.
   e. To strengthen students' composing skills, have them write short pieces in the language they are studying.

7. Music, Drama, and Art
   a. To make students aware that the community provides a range of performances and activities in the arts, have the class prepare and distribute to other students notices regarding such events.
   b. In order that students may keep a record of their progress in a current art project, encourage them to keep a log of what they have achieved during each work session.
   c. To give students practice in writing, have them listen to songs and lyrics of their choice and write in their own words the "message" of the composer.
   d. To help students understand the work of musicians, dramatists, and artists, have these professionals share their art with students; and then give students the opportunity to write about the hard work, the discipline, and the rewards of such performers.
   e. Have students in art appreciation classes describe in writing a painting or other works of art.
   f. Have students write about the feelings and moods they experience when listening to great music.

8. Health and Physical Education
   a. To assess growth, have students keep personal records of their own progress in a particular sport or health project (e.g., a daily diary of jogging), and write comments pertaining to the difficulties they encounter, the methods used to overcome problems that arise, and

Student writing provides valuable information for the teacher about the students' abilities, progress, interests, attitudes, insights, and values.

the goals they set for themselves.

   b. To help students appreciate the effort required in becoming a top athlete or in the challenge of overcoming physical handicaps, have them write about one of the school's star athletes or one of the handicapped students involved in the sports program.

   c. To help students remember important health and safety rules, ask them to record the rules in a notebook and to ask questions about everything they do not understand.

   d. To help students learn more about a particular sport, have them write about it.

9. Family Life and Consumer Affairs

   a. To help students learn to use language for learning, encourage them to keep notebooks to record instructions, plans, safety rules, recipes, questions, and concerns related to the subject matter they are studying.

   b. To help students understand the difficult task that companies have in providing instructions for the general public (e.g., assembling a bicycle), have students write a description for making or assembling an object.

   c. To give students the opportunity to examine their own thoughts and feelings, have them list people who have been important in their lives, and then write about the value of having known these people.

   d. To give students an opportunity to share their experiences in the class with others, ask them to write a pamphlet for students who will be taking the course next semester.

(NOTE: For more information on suggested classroom activities, see the entries in the Selected References for Jack Hailey, James Moffett and Betty Wagner, and Frank O'Hare; also, *Practical Ideas for Teaching Writing as a Process* has detailed descriptions of classroom activities.)

Standards and Expectations for Student Writing

Typically, the standards and expectations regarding student writing are inconsistent from classroom to classroom. What is needed is at least schoolwide agreement in this area. Teachers, administrators, students, and parents must plan together and establish such standards for the whole curriculum, not just for English. Furthermore, they should all realize that written expression requires knowledges and skills which must be taught, not merely expected.

Policies should also be developed and agreed on regarding the assignment and evaluation of homework that involves writing. Typically, during the course of a school day, relatively little time and solitude are available for students to write. Perforce, homework is necessary to extend, supplement, and reinforce student learning in this area. Indeed, since writing is a basic learning tool in all subject matter areas, it should be basic to most homework assignments. However, homework should be assigned on the basis of the needs and abilities of individual students.

Written expression requires knowledges and skills which must be taught, not merely expected.

"Clear thinking becomes clear writing: one can't exist without the other."

William Zinsser

Students, particularly those who plan to further their education at a college or university, need to develop good writing skills. Many institutions of higher education require entering students to have greater competency in writing than they did a few years ago. In fact, the faculties of California's colleges and universities became so concerned that their freshmen were "underprepared" for college-level work that the academic senates of the three public higher educational systems in the state developed the *Statement on Competencies in English and Mathematics Expected of Entering Freshmen.* The work to develop the statement, which began in the spring of 1981, represented the most extensive cooperative activity ever undertaken by the academic senates of the California Community Colleges, the California State University, and the University of California.

The academic senates began their statement by saying, "A substantial number of students who enter California colleges and universities are not prepared for college-level

work." Then they emphasized how important the basic skills were and that "the minimum proficiencies now required for high school graduation are not sufficient to provide" incoming freshmen with the fundamentals they need to succeed in college.

The academic senates said that the reasons for the underpreparation were "varied and complex" but that one of them was a "lack of understanding" among students, parents, and educators of what the competencies were. They recognized that college and university faculties had a responsibility for identifying the competencies and that high school teachers had the responsibility for determining "the methods of instruction by which these competencies can be taught." The academic senates identified the competencies in writing that freshmen should have as follows:

Clarity in writing reflects clarity in thinking. College and university faculty expect students to be able to understand, organize, synthesize, and communicate information, ideas, and opinions. Students must also be able to make critical judgments, to distinguish primary and relevant ideas from those that are subordinate or irrelevant. Students will be required in their college courses to demonstrate these abilities by writing compositions, reports, term papers, and essay examinations. Because the learning process as well as the quality of the student's written work depends upon these abilities, it is crucial that these abilities be developed before students enter college.

Emphasis upon the following writing skills is not meant to diminish the importance of other forms of writing or an appreciation of literature. However, the skills listed below are fundamental for successful baccalaureate-level work.

1. The ability to generate ideas about which to write;

2. The ability to formulate a single statement that clearly expresses the central idea of one's essay;

3. The ability to construct a paragraph that develops and supports the paragraph's main idea with examples or reasons;

4. The ability to organize paragraphs into a logical sequence so that the central idea of the essay is developed to a logical conclusion;

5. The ability to use varied sentence structures and types effectively in order to indicate the meaning, relationship, and the importance of ideas;

6. The ability to write sentences with precise and appropriate words, to distinguish between literal and figurative use of language, and to avoid inappropriate jargon and cliche;

7. The ability to vary one's choice of words and sentences for different audiences and purposes;

8. The ability to present one's own ideas as related to, but clearly distinguished from, the ideas of others, which includes the ability to use documentation and avoid plagiarism;

9. The ability to support one's opinions and conclusions, including the appropriate use of evidence;

10. The ability to use dictionaries and other reference materials for the purpose of checking words and facts used in one's writing; and

11. The ability to proofread one's essay for errors and omissions of both form and substance, to revise and restructure where ideas are poorly organized or where evidence is lacking, to correct the draft for errors in capitalization, spelling, and punctuation, and to produce a finished paper relatively free of sentence fragments, comma splices, agreement errors, and improper pronoun references.[1]

In addition to the action taken by the three academic senates, the Board of Trustees of the California State University also voted to require students entering any of its colleges in the fall of 1984 to have completed four years of college preparatory English. Furthermore, the University specified the criteria for college preparatory English, and among them are the following: "English courses for 11th and 12th graders will be considered college

---

[1]*Statement on Competencies in English and Mathematics Expected of Entering Freshmen.* Prepared by the academic senates of the California Community Colleges, the California State University, and the University of California. Sacramento: The California Round Table on Educational Opportunity, 1982. (Copies of the document are available for $2.50, plus tax for California residents, from Publications Sales, California State Department of Education, P.O. Box 271, Sacramento, CA 95802-0271.)

preparatory if (1) they include writing instruction and evaluation and require substantial amounts of writing of extensive, structured papers, expressive and analytical, demanding a high level of thinking skills; and (2) they are integrated with challenging, in-depth reading of significant literature, either imaginative or analytical, including contemporary or classified works in various genres."

(NOTE: For additional information on standards and expectations, see the material written by Kellogg Hunt that appears in *Evaluating Writing: Describing, Measuring, Judging,* the entry for Richard Graves in the Selected References, and the Department of Education's *Model Curriculum Standards.*)

Teaching Writing to Language Minority Students

The primary and often dominant language of a growing number of students in California's schools is a language other than English, and many of these students have limited proficiency in English. However, it should not be asssumed that the writing program advocated in this handbook is not suitable to the needs of students with limited proficiency in English or that efforts to help them to learn to write well should be delayed until they become fully proficient in English.

No matter what their dominant language might be, all students, including those who might be referred to as language minority students, are more likely to learn to write well if they are familiar with, and engage in, the writing process described earlier in this handbook. Indeed, the process is as appropriate for non-English-speaking students as it is for students whose dominant language is English. Prewriting, writing, responding, revising, editing, developing skills with the conventions of language, evaluating, and postwriting are universally appropriate stages in the writing process.

However, a caveat is in order. *Language minority students* is a broad descriptive phrase that applies to all students who possess varying degrees of proficiency in their primary language and in English. The degree of their proficiency in English and in their primary language determines their readiness to learn to write in English. Thus, it is imperative at the outset for educators to determine the degree of proficiency of language minority students in both English and their primary language.

Proficiency in English, or in any other language for that matter, can be thought of as having two dimensions, which might be referred to as basic and advanced. Basic English is the kind of language which people learn largely in non-school settings. It includes basic abilities to speak, read, and write in English and to understand spoken English. It might be thought of as that level of proficiency in English required for people to function well in their daily encounters with the informal use of the language. Although native speakers of English begin to learn basic English very early in life, those whose primary language is other than English obviously begin the process later.

Advanced English is that kind of language that might be described as academically demanding. It is the predominant dimension of English that students encounter in the classroom or in similar academic settings. Using advanced English requires extensive skills in speaking, reading, and writing English and in understanding spoken English. It is more cognitively demanding than basic English and is the dimension of the language most involved with the writing process.

Students who have not yet attained adequate facility with basic English should not be expected to do well with activities requiring the skills of advanced English. Such students should be provided with a rich array of learning activities designed to improve their proficiency with basic English before they are expected to write extensively in the English language. However, this is not to say that instruction for them in the writing process should be delayed until they attain facility with basic English. The instruction can begin in their dominant language as soon as they have developed a relative mastery of the basic features of that language. Many, and perhaps most, language minority students have developed enough mastery of the basic features of their dominant language to begin writing in that language. Later, as they attain greater proficiency with basic English and with writing in their primary language, they will be able to transfer the skills they have learned in their primary language as they begin to write in English.

For students whose primary language consists of a nonstandard dialect of English, a similar but slightly different approach is in order. Educators should be careful not to confuse nonstandard with substandard. As students are given opportunities to master standard English, there should be no belittling of their dialect. They may be given opportunities to write initially in their own dialect during informal writing activities as a means for developing their interest in the writing process. The use of daily journals is one example of informal writing that might be appropriate. However, since they already have facility with a dialect of English, they should be encouraged to begin to write in standard English as soon as possible. The important thing to keep in mind is that, ultimately, the writing process described earlier is as appropriate to the needs of these students as it is to the needs of any others in developing writing skills.

For language minority students, the prewriting phase is particularly important as they begin to write in English. It is at this point that the interest in writing and the motivation to write in English can be established. They should be given opportunities to try out orally both the form and content of what they wish to say, to ask questions, to solicit words and expressions they need for composing, and to feel free to request assistance. Through the acceptance of students' oral English discourse, however nonstandard it may have been initially, instructors can motivate these students to put their thoughts in writing. Students should be provided with experiences with

"If you write about the things and the people you know best, you discover your roots."

J. Robert Oppenheimer

which they are likely to have early and cumulative success.

Perhaps most importantly of all, the attitude and behavior of instructors should reflect understanding of and respect for students' cultural backgrounds, high expectations for the success of their students, and confidence in the ability of students to ultimately express themselves well in written English. In such a learning environment, students will discover that learning to write is a developmental process during which they gradually refine the language skills they bring to the classroom until they attain adequate facility in writing standard English.

The main focus of this handbook is on the writing process itself and on ways to help all types of students learn to use the process. The special needs of language minority students should be understood and met to the extent that time and resources permit. Bilingual instructional aides, with proper training, can help a great deal in assisting language minority students to learn to write effectively.

"We shape ourselves and our institutions, and we and our institutions are shaped through those individual acts of negotiation between ourselves and our language."

A. Bartlett Giamatti

SUGGESTED ACTIVITIES FOR LANGUAGE MINORITY STUDENTS

1. Provide extensive prewriting activities, such as:
   a. Make use of pictures and interesting objects that can be passed among students to elicit their oral and, ultimately, their written responses.
   b. Make use of rhymes and poetry, especially those with refrains that groups of students can repeat.
   c. Make use of word games, especially those involving elements of humor.
   d. Create stories.
   e. Establish a classroom library of carefully selected and appropriate books and read aloud from them frequently.
   f. Visit sites in the community that are likely to elicit discussion and writing.
   g. Serve various foods as a means for eliciting oral and written responses.
2. Have students compile vocabulary lists of English words that are cognates of words in their primary language.
3. Engage students in group writing to enable each student to make some contribution to the group effort.
4. Urge students to write in their dominant language at the outset and to focus on subjects with which they are familiar.
5. Encourage students to write about their cultural backgrounds.
6. Encourage language minority students initially to write to audiences that are sensitive to their background.
7. Have students write reports on interviews to develop their skills in questioning, transcribing, and editing.

(NOTE: Readers who are particularly concerned about language minority students may wish to seek further information from the entries in the Selected References, especially the entry for Tove Skutnabb-Kangas and from *Schooling and Language Minority Students.*)

Broad Assessments of Student Writing

Often groups within a school, such as high school teachers in an English Department or a group of fifth grade teachers, may wish to evaluate their students' writing abilities. It should be remembered that the purpose of the evaluation should determine the instrument or methods to be used.

The teachers in a science department, for example, might wish to examine their students' writing of laboratory reports on a pretest and post-test basis to determine growth. They would need to make their students aware of their plans, develop a scoring guide, and then evaluate the laboratoary reports for overall organization and clarity. (See page 23 of this handbook.)

Similarly, the teachers of one grade level at a school, might wish to determine their students' abilities to punctuate dialogue. They would need to agree on a testing instrument, test these students, record their scores, and analyze the results. If the staff decides that a schoolwide assessment of some aspect of the writing abilities of students is needed, the scoring and holistic evaluation of samples of their writing would be appropriate.

Schoolwide assessment of student writing plays a key part in helping a school develop an effective writing program. Not only does the assessment provide a record of student growth in writing, but it can also high-

light for students and teachers in the school the centrality of writing in the learning process.

California state law requires the governing board of each school district to establish proficiency standards for all students in basic skill areas, including writing, reading comprehension, and computation. Further, student performance in these areas must be assessed annually at least once in grades four through six, at least once in grades seven through nine, and at least twice in grades ten and eleven.

The proficiency standards required by state law are minimum standards, not ideal standards. In helping as many students as possible attain these minimum standards, educators may lose sight of the larger curricular scene and allow minimum standards to become dominant standards. This handbook can help planners prevent that from happening by assisting them in developing a writing program which meets not only the minimum needs of students but also their writing needs at more sophisticated levels. One intent of the legislation was to ensure that all students attain at least a basic ability to communicate in writing. This handbook can help educational planners design writing programs which ensure that students learn to write as well as they possibly can.

As pointed out earlier in this handbook, properly scored writing samples can reveal not only the degree of proficiency in writing attained by students but can also reveal their specific areas of strength and weakness in both editing and composing. Since student outcomes are what the law focuses on, such information should be of great importance to educators who are attempting to meet the spirit of the law by improving their instructional programs. Accordingly, the use of writing samples for determining students' basic proficiencies in writing is highly recommended.

The use of writing samples for determining students' basic proficiencies in writing is highly recommended.

SUGGESTED ACTIVITIES TO ENHANCE THE BROAD ASSESSMENT OF STUDENT WRITING

1. Plan and execute a schoolwide pretest/post-test of student writing in order to measure the degree of improvement of student writing at all grade levels.
2. Identify specific criteria to be included in the assessment at various grade levels and in each subject area.
3. Provide staff development workshops districtwide to train teachers to score student writing.
4. Have teachers develop a scoring guide for each writing assessment.
5. Include a writing sample in all testing programs that are designed to assess the writing abilities of students.

(NOTE: For additional information on making broad assessments of student writing, see the entries in the Selected References for Charles Cooper and Lee Odell (*Evaluating Writing*), Paul Diederich, Mel Grubb, Miles Myers, Alan Purves, Edward M. White, and the Department of Education's publications on assessment.)

"It took me fifteen years to discover that I had no talent for writing, but I couldn't give it up because by that time I was too famous."

Robert Benchley

IV. Staff Development in the Teaching of Writing

No writing program can be complete or very effective without staff development. Research findings and new methods and materials regarding the teaching of writing are being developed in such quantities today that it is difficult for staff members to stay abreast of the findings and the changes. Furthermore, relatively few teachers received training in the teaching of writing during their pre-service education. Accordingly, appropriate staff development programs are necessary if efforts to improve student writing are to be successful.

Important elements to consider when establishing a staff development program for the teaching of writing include the following:

1. The school staff should participate in planning the program in order to ensure their sense of ownership of the ultimate plan and to ensure that the plan is designed to meet their genuine needs, that the scheduling of staff development efforts is agreed on by potential participants, and that the sources of staff development are respected and supported.
2. Since the teaching of writing is a complex matter, those who plan the staff development programs should design on-going efforts which provide for the necessary periods of time rather than single session or "quick fix" approaches.
3. To the degree possible, staff development efforts in the teaching of writing should occur during the regular working hours of teachers rather than after school or on weekends.
4. Those who conduct staff development programs in the teaching of writing should be trained for the task. The programs they offer should be grounded on research findings and should provide teachers with practical information as to how to apply the findings in their teaching.
5. The simple passing of information about effective ways to teach writing should merely be an early step in a staff development program in this area. To ensure that teachers learn how to improve their teaching of writing and that such improvement leads to improved student performance in writing, it is imperative that subsequent steps be taken. Participating teachers should:
   a. Watch demonstrations of the teaching of newly acquired concepts and approaches in the teaching of writing.

39

No writing program can be complete or very effective without staff development.

b. Incorporate these concepts and approaches in their own teaching.

c. Have opportunities to share ideas in the teaching of writing with colleagues and to learn from them.

d. Have informed and trusted peers visit their classrooms to ensure that they understand the new concepts and approaches and are employing them effectively in their own teaching.

6. Teachers should have conveniently available to them a professional library regarding the teaching of writing. (Teachers and librarians could use the Selected References in this handbook as a checklist for determining the adequacy of their libraries.) Furthermore, procedures should be established to ensure that the library is kept up to date, especially in terms of ongoing research.

7. The staff development effort should receive the obvious support of district and school site administrators.

8. Efforts should be made to enlist the support of the local school district governing board and the public for the staff development program. It is particularly important to ensure that staff development be considered important

enough so that part of the staff's professional time is reserved for the program.

9. Teachers should be encouraged to participate in professional organizations, meetings, workshops, and conferences that are likely to enhance their skills and knowledge regarding the teaching of writing.

10. Administrators and other nonteaching school staff members should support staff development efforts in the teaching of writing and, to the degree possible, participate in the program.

11. Teachers should receive staff development in writing. They should be encouraged to engage frequently in the same writing assignments they give to their students. By doing so, they serve as models, they discover potential roadblocks or unnecessary difficulties in the wording of an assignment, they become more aware of what students go through when writing, and they become more aware of the importance of the content and not the mere mechanics of written expression.

Information may be found in the appendix about the California Writing Project, a statewide staff development program in California that should be helpful to those who wish to design inservice education programs at the local level.

V. Checklist
for Assessing a School's Writing Program

The following checklist is based on the foregoing text. However, further reading and the examination of local programs for teaching writing may encourage those who decide to use this checklist to augment it. Perforce, it is not exhaustive. Neither is it intended as a teacher evaluation instrument.

Readers should think of this checklist as a tool for examining a school's overall program for teaching students to write. It is intended to help those who are concerned about the teaching of writing at a school site to become fully aware of the strengths and weaknesses of the existing program and the need for possible changes.

If improperly used, checklists can be intimidating and ultimately counterproductive. To avoid this possible outcome, those who decide to use this checklist are urged to read all of the preceding text. They might also consider readings from the Selected References and the publications of the California State Department of Education. Finally, they might consider establishing a spirit of collegiality at a school site level regarding the assessment of the school's writing program. If a sense of ownership of solutions to possible areas of need can be established, the use of assessment instruments, such as this checklist, will be far less threatening.

"Where there is much desire to learn, there of necessity will be much arguing, much writing, many opinions; for opinion in good men is but knowledge in the making."

John Milton

I. Motivation for Students to Write (See page 6 in the text.)

How effective is your writing program in providing for:

	Ineffective	Somewhat effective	Effective	Very effective
1. Schoolwide encouragement for teachers to engage occasionally in the same writing assignments they ask of their students?				
2. Opportunities for students to address topics appropriate to their interests and levels of knowledge?				
3. Prewriting activities?				
4. Positive reactions by teachers to anything in the writing process that students do well?				
5. The avoidance of excessive attention to correctness early in the process of teaching students to write?				
6. Opportunities for students to watch adults engage in the writing process?				

II. The Writing Process

A. Prewriting—the First Stage (See page 11 in the text.)

How effective is your writing program in providing for:

	Ineffective	Somewhat effective	Effective	Very effective
1. Time for students to reflect and to develop their confidence and fluency?	___	___	___	___
2. Time for students to define an audience during the prewriting stage?	___	___	___	___
3. A variety of prewriting experiences, such as displays of student work, brainstorming, clustering, dramatic activities, field trips, interviewing, and the use of audiovisual materials?	___	___	___	___
4. Opportunities for students to talk to each other and to the teacher about their writing and their plans for writing?	___	___	___	___
5. A classroom environment with sufficient space and materials to stimulate writing activities?	___	___	___	___

B. Writing—One Stage in the Process (See page 13 in the text.)

Writing to Develop Fluency

How effective is your writing program in providing for:

	Ineffective	Somewhat effective	Effective	Very effective
1. Both individual and group writing activities?	___	___	___	___
2. Oral language experiences as a precursor to writing, especially for beginners and for language minority students?	___	___	___	___
3. Occasional experiences that allow students to write without having to be concerned about evaluation, editing, or critiques?	___	___	___	___
4. Occasional writing experiences designed to promote quantity of production quickly at a single sitting?	___	___	___	___
5. Opportunities for students to gain confidence in the value and supply of their own ideas by writing in such forms as stream-of-consciousness writing, sensory reporting, diaries, journals, learning logs, and dialogues?	___	___	___	___
6. Occasional writing experiences in all curricular areas?	___	___	___	___

II. The Writing Process—Continued

How effective is your writing program in providing for:

	Ineffective	Somewhat effective	Effective	Very effective
7. Writing experiences for which students know they will be the sole audience?				
8. Opportunities for students to dictate to another person who records their first draft?				

Writing for an Audience

How effective is your writing program in providing for:

	Ineffective	Somewhat effective	Effective	Very effective
1. Opportunities for students to write for various audiences, other than the teacher, including egocentric writing, such as entries in journals and diaries?				
2. Learning opportunities to help students realize the importance of identifying their audiences before they begin to write?				
3. Opportunities to improve students' sense of audience by writing in various modes, such as letters (to a business firm, to an editor, to friends and family, and so forth), essays, reports, announcements, brief narratives and descriptions, articles, plays, poems, biographies, autobiographies, instructions, research papers, and news stories?				
4. Opportunities to improve their sense of audience by writing about the same subject in different forms, as appropriate, to several different audiences?				

Writing with Purpose

How effective is your writing program in providing for:

	Ineffective	Somewhat effective	Effective	Very effective
1. Opportunities for students to write for a variety of purposes?				
2. Opportunities for students to study various models of writing which exemplify differing purposes for writing?				
3. Encouragement for students to determine the purpose of their writing during the prewriting stage?				
4. Encouragement for students to reconsider during the revision stage the purpose of what they have written?				

II. The Writing Process—Continued

How effective is your writing program in providing for:

	Ineffective	Somewhat effective	Effective	Very effective
5. Assignments in which students are directed to determine the author's purpose in various reading selections?	___	___	___	___
6. Assignments in which students write to several different audiences with a single purpose in mind and to a single audience for varied purposes?	___	___	___	___

C. Responding—Reacting to What Was Written (See page 16 in the text.)

How effective is your writing program in providing for:

	Ineffective	Somewhat effective	Effective	Very effective
1. Opportunities for students to help and support each other by exchanging written and oral responses to their writing?	___	___	___	___
2. Class sessions during which the better sections of students' work is read aloud for the enjoyment and enlightenment of the class and for purposes of illustrating what constitutes better writing?	___	___	___	___
3. Encouragement for students to monitor their own writing development through a periodic review of their papers?	___	___	___	___
4. Responses to student writing which focus on its content before attention is directed to problems students may have with the conventions of writing?	___	___	___	___

D. Revising—Reexamining What Was Written (See page 18 in the text.)

How effective is your writing program in providing for:

	Ineffective	Somewhat effective	Effective	Very effective
1. Opportunities for students to revise papers based on the responses of teachers, peers, or others before the papers are formally evaluated?	___	___	___	___
2. Instruction in revision skills, such as adding detail and omitting repetition?	___	___	___	___
3. Opportunities for reconsidering such matters as point of view, tone, voice, and audience?	___	___	___	___
4. Practice with the four revision skills of addition, deletion, substitution, and rearrangement?	___	___	___	___

II. The Writing Process—Continued

E. Editing—Refining What Was Written (See page 19 in the text.)

How effective is your writing program in providing for:

	Ineffective	Somewhat effective	Effective	Very effective
1. Opportunities for students and teachers to distinguish between revision and editing?				
2. Opportunities for students to learn to edit their work for the conventions of writing, including grammar, usage, capitalization, punctuation, spelling, paragraphing, and proper manuscript format?				
3. Opportunities for students to learn to edit their work for errors in diction and syntax?				
4. Opportunities for students to learn to understand that editing is the final step in refining their papers?				

F. Developing Skill with the Conventions of Writing (See page 20 in the text.)

How effective is your writing program in providing for:

	Ineffective	Somewhat effective	Effective	Very effective
1. Learning opportunities regarding the conventions of writing as the need arises during actual writing activities, rather than isolating them and treating them as a prerequisite to writing instruction?				
2. The evaluation of students' mastery of the conventions of writing on the basis of their writing samples rather than relying solely on objective tests covering these conventions?				
3. Opportunities for students to explore the potential of the English language and to experiment with a variety of ways of correctly expressing their ideas?				
4. Opportunities for students to present their work to a group of peers for responses, with the option of revising and correcting before submission for evaluation?				
5. Early identification of students' needs regarding the conventions of writing?				

II. The Writing Process—Continued

G. Evaluating—Judging the Writing Constructively (See page 21 in the text.)

How effective is your writing program in providing for:

	Ineffective	Somewhat effective	Effective	Very effective
1. Self-evaluation at each stage in the composing process?	___	___	___	___
2. Strategies that will prepare students to evaluate their own writing?	___	___	___	___
3. Peer evaluation of each student's writing?	___	___	___	___
4. Training to enable students to evaluate effectively the writing of their peers?	___	___	___	___
5. The determination of the purpose of an evaluation effort?	___	___	___	___
6. The selection of the most appropriate means for conducting an evaluation, such as holistic, analytical, or primary trait scoring?	___	___	___	___
7. Policies that reflect consistent and regular assessment of varied writing tasks?	___	___	___	___
8. The use of student writing samples as a primary means of evaluating their writing?	___	___	___	___
9. Teacher staff development in the evaluation of student writing?	___	___	___	___

H. Postwriting—Realizing the Importance of Writing (See page 23 in the text.)

How effective is your writing program in providing for:

	Ineffective	Somewhat effective	Effective	Very effective
1. The publication of student writing in all curriculum areas in class or school magazines, newspapers, or books?	___	___	___	___
2. Frequent schoolwide recognition of sucessful writing by students at all ability levels through public displays, interclass or interschool exchanges, awards, and assemblies?	___	___	___	___
3. Opportunities for students to receive responses from audiences other than the teacher?	___	___	___	___
4. Opportunities for students to enter school, district, community, and national writing competitions?	___	___	___	___

II. The Writing Process—Continued

How effective is your writing program in providing for:

		Ineffective	Somewhat effective	Effective	Very effective
5.	Opportunities for students to write and mail letters to friends, relatives, companies, editors, celebrities, political figures, and other audiences?	___	___	___	___

III. Implementing a Schoolwide Writing Program

A. General Considerations for a Schoolwide Writing Program (See page 25 in the text.)

How effective is your writing program in providing for:

		Ineffective	Somewhat effective	Effective	Very effective
1.	The preparation of a written plan for a schoolwide writing program?	___	___	___	___
2.	Schoolwide agreement on the objectives for teaching writing?	___	___	___	___
3.	Schoolwide agreement that writing is an important tool for learning in all subjects?	___	___	___	___
4.	Schoolwide agreement that teachers in all content areas at the secondary level have responsibilities to assist with the teaching of writing?	___	___	___	___
5.	The encouragement of student writing in all subject areas at the elementary school level?	___	___	___	___
6.	The clarification of the purposes and methods for evaluating writing in all content areas?	___	___	___	___
7.	Adequate time for writing in all content areas?	___	___	___	___
8.	In-service education programs on the teaching of writing for *all* teachers?	___	___	___	___
9.	The involvement of school administrators in the writing program?	___	___	___	___
10.	Activities designed to help beginners make the transition from oral to written language?	___	___	___	___
11.	Activities designed to elicit student writing in each of the specific subject matter areas included in the school's curriculum?	___	___	___	___

III. Implementing a Schoolwide Writing Program—Continued

B. Standards and Expectations for Student Writing (See page 31 in the text.)

How effective is your writing program in providing for:

	Ineffective	Somewhat effective	Effective	Very effective
1. The establishment of schoolwide standards regarding the quality of student writing and homework involving writing?	___	___	___	___
2. Opportunities that will enable students and parents to become aware of these adopted standards?	___	___	___	___
3. Uniform schoolwide application of these standards?	___	___	___	___
4. The establishment of grading policies regarding student work that is in accord with these standards?	___	___	___	___
5. A schoolwide effort to help college-bound students gain the writing skills they need?	___	___	___	___

C. Teaching Writing to Language Minority Students (See page 34 in the text.)

How effective is your writing program in encouraging schoolwide efforts in the following:

	Ineffective	Somewhat effective	Effective	Very effective
1. Determining the levels of proficiency that language minority students have in both their dominant language and in English?	___	___	___	___
2. Helping language minority students develop skills with the basic features of their dominant language before they are required to write?	___	___	___	___
3. Development of "basic English" skills of language minority students before requiring them to write in English? (See page 34 for a definition of "basic English.")	___	___	___	___
4. Encouragement for students who have not yet attained facility with "basic English," but who have attained facility with the basic features of their dominant language, to learn about and make use of the stages in the writing process by writing in their dominant language initially?	___	___	___	___
5. Encouragement of students who have begun to attain facility with "basic English" to transfer the skills they have learned and to begin to write in English?	___	___	___	___

III. Implementing a Schoolwide Writing Program—Continued

How effective is your writing program in encouraging schoolwide efforts in the following:

	Ineffective	Somewhat effective	Effective	Very effective
6. Provision for appropriate staff development for those who are responsible for helping language minority students learn to write in English?	___	___	___	___
7. Development of appropriate attitudes and behaviors on the part of all who work with language minority students?	___	___	___	___
8. Avoidance of any belittling of students' dominant language, dialect, or culture?	___	___	___	___
9. Extensive prewriting activities and small group work for language minority students?	___	___	___	___
10. Extensive oral language activities for language minority students?	___	___	___	___

IV. Staff Development in the Teaching of Writing (See page 39 in the text.)

How effective is your writing program in providing for:

	Ineffective	Somewhat effective	Effective	Very effective
1. Participation by school staff members in planning and implementing a staff development program in the teaching of writing?	___	___	___	___
2. Staff development programs which are ongoing?	___	___	___	___
3. Staff development programs which occur during the regular teaching day rather than during off-duty time?	___	___	___	___
4. The adequacy of staff development trainers in the area of writing?	___	___	___	___
5. Opportunities for participating teachers to experience demonstration teaching, to share ideas with colleagues, and to receive classroom visits and coaching from informed and trusted peers to ensure that they are using newly acquired skills and knowledge in their teaching?	___	___	___	___
6. A professional library on the teaching of writing?	___	___	___	___

IV. Staff Development in the Teaching of Writing —Continued

How effective is your writing program in providing for:

	Ineffec-tive	Some-what effec-tive	Effec-tive	Very effec-tive
7. Adequate support for staff development in the teaching of writing by district and school site administrators, the school board, and the public?				
8. Encouragement for teachers of writing to participate in appropriate professional organizations, workshops, and conferences?				
9. The involvement of administrators and other non-teaching staff members in staff development efforts to improve student writing?				

Appropriate staff development programs are necessary if efforts to improve student writing are to be successful.

How to Help Your Child Become a Better Writer

Suggestions for Parents from the National Council of Teachers of English

(Reprinted by Permission)

Dear Parent:

We're pleased you want to know how to help the NCTE effort to improve the writing of young people. Parents and teachers working together are the best means for assuring that children and youth will become skillful writers.

Because the situation in every home is different, we can't say when the best time is to pursue each of the following suggestions. In any case, please be aware that writing skill develops slowly. For some, it comes early; for others it comes late. Occasionally, a child's skill may even seem to go backwards. Nonetheless, with your help and encouragement, the child will certainly progress.

The members of the National Council of Teachers of English welcome your involvement in your child's education in writing. We hope you will enjoy following these suggestions for helping your child become a better writer, both at home and at school.

Things to Do at Home

1. Build a climate of words at home. Go places and see things with your child; then talk about what has been seen, heard, smelled, tasted, touched. The basis of good writing is good talk, and younger children especially grow into stronger control of language when loving adults—particularly parents—share experiences and rich talk about those experiences.

2. Let children see you write often. You're both a model and a teacher. If children never see adults write, they gain an impression that writing occurs only at school. What you *do* is as important as what you say. Have children see you writing notes to friends, letters to business firms, perhaps stories to share with the children. From time to time, read aloud what you have written and ask the children their opinion of what you've said. If it's not perfect, so much the better. Making changes in what you write confirms for the child that revision is a natural part of writing, which it is.

3. Be as helpful as you can in helping children write. Talk through their ideas with them; help them discover what they want to say. When they ask for help with spelling, punctuation, and usage, supply that help. Your most effective role is not as a critic but as a helper. Rejoice in effort, delight in ideas, and resist the temptation to be critical.

4. Provide a suitable place for children to write. A quiet corner is best, the child's own place, if possible. If not, any flat surface

Your most effective role is not as a critic but as a helper.

with elbow room, a comfortable chair, and a good light will do.

5. Give, and encourage others to give, the child gifts associated with writing:
   - pens of several kinds
   - pencils of appropriate size and hardness
   - a desk lamp
   - pads of paper, stationery, and envelopes—even stamps
   - a booklet for a diary or daily journal (Make sure that the booklet is the child's private property; when children want to share, they will.)
   - a dictionary appropriate to the child's age and needs. Most dictionary use is for checking spelling, but a good dictionary contains fascinating information on word origins, synonyms, pronunciation, and so forth.
   - a thesaurus for older children. This will help in the search for the "right" word.
   - a typewriter, even a battered portable will do, allowing for occasional public messages, like neighborhood newspapers, play scripts
   - erasers or "white-out" liquid for correcting errors that the child wants to repair without rewriting.

6. Encourage (but do not demand) frequent writing. Be patient with reluctance to write. "I have nothing to say" is a perfect excuse. Recognize that the desire to write is a sometime thing. There will be times when a child "burns" to write, others when the need is cool. But frequency of writing is important to develop the habit of writing.

7. Praise the child's efforts at writing. Forget what happened to you in school, and resist the tendency to focus on errors of spelling, punctuation, and other mechanical parts of writing. Emphasize the child's successes. For every error the child makes, there are dozens of things he or she has done well.

8. Share letters from friends and relatives. Treat such letters as special events. Urge relatives and friends to write notes and letters to the child, no matter how brief. Writing is especially rewarding when the child gets a response. When thank you notes are in order, after a holiday especially, sit with the child and write your own notes at the same time. Writing ten letters (for ten gifts) is a heavy burden for the child; space the work and be supportive.

9. Encourage the child to write away for information, free samples, travel brochures. For a great many suggestions about where to write and how to write, purchase a copy of the helpful U.S. Postal Service booklet, *All About Letters* (available from NCTE @ $1.50 per copy).

10. Be alert to occasions when the child can be involved in writing. For example, helping with grocery lists; adding notes at the end of parents' letters; sending holiday and birthday cards; taking down telephone messages; writing notes to friends; helping plan trips by writing for information; drafting notes to school for parental signature; writing notes to letter carriers and other service persons; preparing invitations to family get-togethers.

Writing for real purposes is rewarding, and the daily activities of families present many opportunities for purposeful writing. Involving your child may take some coaxing, but it will be worth your patient effort.

Things to Do for School Writing Programs

1. Ask to see the child's writing, either the writing brought home or the writing kept in folders at school. Encourage the use of writing folders, both at home and at school. Most writing should be kept, not thrown away. Folders are important means for helping

Praise the child's efforts at writing.

both teachers and children see progress in writing skill.

2. Be affirmative about the child's efforts in school writing. Recognize that for every error a child makes, he or she will do many things right. Applaud the good things you see. The willingness to write is fragile. Your optimistic attitude toward the child's efforts is vital to strengthening the writing habit.

3. Be primarily interested in the content, not the mechanics of expression. It's easy for many adults to spot misspellings, faulty word usage, and shaky punctuation. Perfection in these escapes most adults, so don't demand it of children. Sometimes teachers— for these same reasons—will mark only a few mechanical errors, leaving others for another time. What matters most in writing is words, sentences, and ideas. Perfection in mechanics develops slowly. Be patient.

4. Find out if children are given writing instruction and practice in writing on a regular basis. Daily writing is the ideal; once a week is not often enough. If classes are too large in your school, understand that it may not be possible for teachers to ask for as much writing practice as they or you would like. Insist on smaller classes—no more than 25 in elementary schools and no more than four classes of 25 for secondary school English teachers.

5. Ask if *every* teacher is involved in helping youngsters write better. Work sheets, blank filling exercises, multiple choice tests, and similar materials are sometimes used to *avoid* having children write. If children and youth are not being asked to write sentences and paragraphs about science, history, geography, and the other school subjects, they are not being helped to become better writers. *All* teachers have responsibility to help children improve their writing skills.

6. See if youngsters are being asked to write in a variety of forms (letters, essays, stories, etc.) for a variety of purposes (to inform, persuade, describe, etc.) and for a variety of audiences (other students, teachers, friends, strangers, relatives, business firms). Each form, purpose, and audience demands differences of style, tone, approach, and choice of words. A wide variety of writing experiences is critical to developing effective writing.

7. Check to see if there is continuing contact with the imaginative writing of skilled authors. While it's true we learn to write by writing, we also learn to write by reading. The works of talented authors should be studied not only for ideas but also for the writing skills involved. Good literature is an essential part of any effective writing program.

8. Watch out for "the grammar trap." Some people may try to persuade you that a full understanding of English grammar is needed before students can express themselves well. Some knowledge of grammar *is* useful, but too much time spent on the study of grammar steals time from the

Be primarily interested in the content, not the mechanics of expression.

study of writing. Time is much better spent in writing and conferring with the teacher or other students about each attempt to communicate in writing.

9. Encourage administrators to see that teachers of writing have plenty of supplies—writing paper, teaching materials, duplicating and copying machines, dictionaries, books about writing, and classroom libraries of good books.

10. Work through your PTA and your school board to make writing a high priority. Learn about writing and the ways youngsters learn to write. Encourage publication of good student writing in school newspapers, literary journals, local newspapers, and magazines. See that the high school's best writers are entered into the NCTE Achievement Awards in Writing Program or the Scholastic Writing Awards or other writing contests. Let everyone know that writing matters to you.

By becoming an active participant in your child's education as a writer, you will serve not only your child but other children and youth as well. You have an important role to play, and we encourage your involvement.

For additional copies of this brochure, send requests prepaid to the NCTE Order Department, 1111 Kenyon Road, Urbana, IL 61801. Up to 14, free; 15—99, $.05 each; 100 or more, $4.50 per hundred. Parents and teachers are encouraged to make copies for use with local groups. The brochure is also available in Spanish from NCTE.

"A sentence should contain no unnecessary words, a paragraph no unnecessary sentences, for the same reason that a drawing should have no unnecessary lines and a machine no unnecessary parts."

William Strunk, Jr.

The California Writing Project

With the help of the California State Department of Education, the Bay Area Writing Project, which was begun in 1974 by the University of California, Berkeley, has been expanded during the last few years and has become known as the California Writing Project. A distinctive feature of this project is the collaboration it has fostered among disparate participating agencies.

The projects that make up the California Writing Project have enjoyed the support, joint planning, and involvement of educators from school districts, offices of county superintendents of schools, the State Department of Education, community colleges, and public and private colleges and universities. Instead of haggling over where to place blame for the problem of poor writing by students, representatives of these various educational organizations have engaged in wholesome dialogue, have established working relationships, and have cooperatively established these new writing projects.

Central to these projects is the selection and training of cadres of teachers of writing. Those teachers then serve as in-service education leaders and change agents in their own and other schools and institutions of higher education. Annually at each project center, approximately 25 carefully selected instructors, from the elementary through the university levels, spend six weeks during the summer as University Fellows. They are intensively trained to teach effectively the composing process to students and also to their peers.

During the subsequent year they continue with their regular teaching but then become known as teacher consultants. Project personnel negotiate with the employers of the teacher consultants to obtain the occasional release of the consultants to conduct in-service education programs.

Since the inception of the project, several hundred educators have received summer training. They, in turn, have provided in-service education for hundreds of others whose new knowledge has enabled them to improve their teaching of the composing process.

General information about the California Writing Project may be secured from the University of California, Berkeley/Bay Area Writing Project or from:

Language Arts/Foreign Language Unit
California State Department of Education
P.O. Box 944272
Sacramento, CA 94244-2720
(916) 322-3285

The California Writing Project is composed of the following:

Area III Writing Project
English Department, Sproul Hall
University of California, Davis
Davis, CA 95616
(916) 752-8394 or 752-8392

California State University, Northridge Writing Project
Department of English
California State University, Northridge
18111 Nordhoff
Northridge, CA 91330
(213) 885-3431

The Bay Area Writing Project ". . . appears to be the best large scale effort to improve composition instruction now in operation in this country, and certainly is the best on which substantial data are available."

Michael Scriven

California Writing Project, UC-Irvine
Office of Teacher Education
University of California, Irvine
Irvine, CA 92717
(714) 856-7842 or 856-6781

Central California Writing Project
Oakes College
University of California, Santa Cruz
Santa Cruz, CA 95064
(408) 429-2813

Central Coast Writing Project
English Department
California Polytechnic State University
San Luis Obispo, CA 93407
(805) 546-2400 or 546-2596

CSULB/South Basin Writing Project
English Department
California State University, Long Beach
1250 Bellflower Blvd.
Long Beach, CA 90840
(213) 498-4223

Great Valley Writing Project
Office of the Stanislaus County
    Superintendent of Schools
801 County Center Three Court
Modesto, CA 95355
(209) 571-6605

Instead of haggling over where to place blame for the problem of poor writing by students, representatives of these various educational organizations have engaged in wholesome dialogue, have established working relationships, and have cooperatively established these new writing projects.

Inland Area Writing Project
Department of English
California State University, San Bernardino
5500 University Parkway
San Bernardino, CA 92407
(714) 887-7446

School of Education
University of California, Riverside
Riverside, CA 92521
(714) 787-4361

Kern/Eastern Sierra Writing Project
School of Education
California State College, Bakersfield
9001 Stockdale Highway
Bakersfield, CA 93309
(805) 833-2379 or 833-2219

Northern California Writing Project
Department of English
California State University, Chico
Chico, CA 95926
(916) 895-5840 or 895-5124

Redwood Writing Project
English Department
Humboldt State University
Arcata, CA 95521
(707) 826-9725

San Diego Area Writing Project
School of Education
University of San Diego
Alcala Park
San Diego, CA 92111
(619) 260-4538

University of California,
    San Diego
D-009, Third College Humanities
    Building, Room 133
La Jolla, CA 92093
(619) 452-2576

San Joaquin Valley Writing Project
Department of English
California State University, Fresno
Fresno, CA 93740
(209) 294-2553

Sonoma State University/North Bay Area
    Writing Project
English Department
Sonoma State University
Rohnert Park, CA 94928
(707) 664-2140

South Bay Writing Project
English Department
San Jose State University
San Jose, CA 95192
(408) 277-2817

South Coast Writing Project
Department of English
University of California
Santa Barbara, CA 93106
(805) 961-2510

UCLA Writing Project
Galey Center, Suite 304
University of California
Los Angeles, CA 90024
(213) 825-2531

University of California, Berkeley/Bay
    Area Writing Project
School of Education
5635 Tolman Hall
University of California
Berkeley, CA 94720
(415) 642-0963

USC/California Writing Project
USC Writing Project—HSS 200
University of Southern California
Los Angeles, CA 90089-0062
(213) 743-4942

APPENDIX C

Computers in the Curriculum

By Stephen Marcus

EDITOR'S NOTE: This article, which appeared in the October, 1984, issue of *Electronic Learning* (copyright, 1984, all rights reserved), was written by Stephen Marcus, Associate Director of the South Coast Writing Project (SCWriP) at the University of California, Santa Barbara. The article is reproduced here by permission of the author and the publisher, Scholastic, Inc., 730 Broadway, New York, NY 10003. SCWriP is one of the California Writing Projects, which are described in Appendix B.

What purpose does writing serve in the schools? The first and most obvious answer is for students to record what they know in term papers, book reports, essay tests, and so forth. A very different—and equally valuable—purpose for writing is to help students discover what it is they can learn. In the act of trying to put things into words, students can discover their ideas, sharpen their thoughts, and order their thinking.

Today, there are numerous software resources available to help students acquire the skills necessary for both purposes in writing. This software for computer-assisted instruction in writing (CAI/writing) ranges from the earliest, single-activity, drill-and-practice software to the notion of "idea processors," and can best be described in terms of "generations."

First Generation: Drill

The earliest application of computers to writing instruction and the composing process was in the area of drill and practice. This group of programs focuses on basic skills such as spelling, punctuation, or sentence combining. Well designed drill-and-practice software provides instruction that takes advantage of the computer's capacity for presenting information in a compelling and interactive way while also keeping track of the students' progress.

Although first-generation CAI/writing will undoubtedly continue to improve in its capacity for instructing and refining students' basic skills, it is with the introduction of second generation software that the computer begins to have a more profound effect on writing.

Second Generation: Writer Aids

Whether the writer's purpose is to record or to discover, the composing process is often thought of in terms of a simple prewriting-writing-rewriting model. Research has shown that most writers spend 85 percent of their time on prewriting (thinking, talking, making notes, outlining, and brainstorming); 1 percent on writing (putting down the first complete version); and 14 percent on rewriting (proofreading, minor editing, and major rethinking). The term "writer aids" refers to the second-generation software that focuses on one of these three stages of the composing process.

Prewriting programs. Several useful approaches to computer-assisted prewriting allow students to generate preliminary ideas and structures for literary analysis, expository essays, or poems. In general, the computer presents the student with a coherent set of questions modeled on those that a teacher might use to elicit the student's own ideas. In some cases, stu-

57

dents' responses are put in an appropriate format; in others, the computer merely provides a printout of the resulting "dialogue," providing the student with raw material for a draft.

Word processors. These are the tools for turning computers into text editors, making it possible to add, delete, change, or move text with just a few keystrokes.

Text analyzers. A third kind of writer's aid is found in software that will analyze the student's style and provide feedback on such dimensions as the degree of sexist language, jargon, or imprecise diction. Especially sophisticated software may check on subject-verb agreement and use of active or passive voice. Various programs will check spelling and punctuation. An ever increasing number of programs will suggest changes and will provide direct instruction to help students make appropriate revisions.

It should be remembered that second-generation software generally focuses on a single stage of the composing process. The prewriting software has virtually no word processing capability. Word processors may help you search and replace, but they won't help you figure out what to put there in the first place.

Third Generation: Integration

It was inevitable that developers would produce software with integrated capacities. Programs like *Quill* (DCH Educational Software, D.C. Heath and Co., Lexington, Massachusetts), *WANDAH* (Ruth Von Blum, Venice, California), *The Writer's Helper* (Conduit, Iowa City, Iowa), and *The Writer's Workshop* (Milliken, St. Louis, Missouri) are examples of

courseware that has evolved from earlier focus on each stage of the composing process. Such programs that provide direct instruction in prewriting include a word processor and have editing and rewriting aids.

The Model Expanded

This working model of the writing process is often expanded to include the getting of readers' reactions prior to revision and the "publication" of students' writing, either formally or in the more general sense of "making it public," for example by reading it out loud to classmates or by posting it for others to read.

Computers provide specialized means for generating, storing, and revising texts. They also allow groups of people to have easy access to each other's work and allow teachers to examine the various stages of the students' writing in progress. Many

Invisible Writing: A Classroom Computer Activity

A different kind of computer-assisted prewriting—one that doesn't require specialized software—demonstrates one of the unique qualities of the technology. This is the "invisible writing with computers" approach developed by the South Coast Writing Project at the University of California, Santa Barbara.

By turning down the monitor's brightness knob, students could not see their prewriting, even though their evolving text was being recorded by the word processor they were using. Students reported that invisible writing allowed them to resist premature proofreading and, hence, they were better able to "understand that writing really begins with prewriting."

This is a simple trick to play with the computer, yet it suggests how word processors themselves, as tools for the writing stage of the composing process, have *instructional* dimensions. They teach students that writing isn't what it used to be: excruciating preparation for tedious revision and retyping. Students see that their words are no longer "carved in stone." They are instead written in light, a fluid medium that offers little resistance to physical manipulation.

teachers have developed informal ways to have comments added to students' word processor files, and specially designed software like *RSVP* (Kamala Anandam, Miami, Florida) allows teachers to "mark up" papers in traditional red-pen fashion.

In addition to these more traditional approaches, there is the growing availability of telecommunications networks that provide students with the chance to get real responses to their writing from real readers—sometimes readers with radically different backgrounds and expectations. One striking example is the correspondence arranged between elementary students in southern California and their counterparts in Alaska. Using software called *The Writer's Assistant* (James Levin, Cardiff by the Sea, California) along with a telecommunications system, the students have been able to experience the fascination and frustration of making themselves clear. (For a detailed discussion of this project, see *Electronic Learning*, May/June, 1984, p. 48.)

Additional Approaches

Finally, there is specialized software like *Story Tree* (Scholastic Inc., New York City) that students and teachers can use to create interactive stories—stories in which readers choose one of several possible story lines. Other software like *Think Tank* (Living Video Text, Palo Alto, California) and *Max Think* (230 Crocker Ave., Piedmont, CA 94610) helps organize ideas in a traditional outline form, but the software aids the writer in deciding how to categorize particular ideas. Other programs, still in development, will help students generate and test hypotheses.

It seems clear that future software will refine and extend existing approaches to CAI/writing. The trend toward integrated packages will perhaps come to include specific routines for acquiring open-ended human response as well as programmed machine analyses. More readily available data bases will perhaps encourage student writers to browse through electronic libraries and to increase their interest in more traditional ones.

As many advances as there have been in CAI/writing, it's well to remember that—"generations" notwithstanding—the field is in its infancy. The field is fortunate, however, in that it has plenty of good models to choose from in the instructional arena and exciting development tools to adopt from the technological domain. Most important, however, is that very talented teachers all over the nation are combining the best of both worlds to the benefit of themselves and their students.

Selected References

A great deal has been published regarding the teaching of writing, especially during recent years. However, only those books and periodicals that are cited in the text and that are particularly pertinent to the content of this handbook appear here. Many noteworthy publications on the subject are not listed, but only because they did not seem immediately appropriate for the handbook's purposes. Selected publications of the California State Department of Education, including those cited in the text, are listed on page 71.

Books

Applebee, Arthur. *The Child's Concept of Story: Ages Two to Seventeen.* Chicago: University of Chicago Press, 1978.

Applebee, Arthur. *Writing in the Secondary School: English and the Content Areas.* Urbana, Ill.: National Council of Teachers of English, 1981.

Berthoff, Ann E. *Forming-Thinking-Writing: The Composing Imagination.* Montclair, N.J.: Boynton/Cook Publishers, Inc., 1982.

Berthoff, Ann E. *The Making of Meaning: Metaphors, Models, and Maxims for Writing Teachers.* Montclair, N.J.: Boynton/Cook Publishers, Inc., 1981.

Blount, Nathan S. "Research on Teaching Literature, Language and Composition," in *Second Handbook of Research on Teaching.* Edited by Robert M. W. Travers. Chicago: Rand McNally and Co., 1973.

Braddock, Richard, and others. *Research in Written Composition.* Urbana, Ill.: National Council of Teachers of English, 1963.

Brande, Dorothea. *Becoming A Writer.* Los Angeles: J. P. Tarcher, 1981. (Distributed by St. Martin's Press).

Brannon, Lil; Melinda Knight; and Vara Neverow-Turk. *Writers Writing.* Montclair, N.J.: Boynton/Cook Publishers, Inc., 1982.

Britton, James, and others. *The Development of Writing Abilities (11-18).* Basingstoke, Hampshire: Macmillan Education Ltd., 1975.

Buckley, Marilyn, and Owen Boyle. *Mapping the Writing Journey.* Berkeley: Bay Area Writing Project, University of California, Berkeley, 1981.[1]

Caplan, Rebekah, and Catharine Keech. *Showing Writing: A Training Program to Help Students Be Specific.* Berkeley: Bay Area Writing Project, University of California, Berkeley, 1980.

The Chicago Manual of Style (Thirteenth edition, revised). Chicago: The University of Chicago Press, 1982.

Christensen, Francis, and Bonniejean Christensen. *Notes Toward a New Rhetoric: Nine Essays for Teachers* (Second edition). New York: Harper & Row Publishers, Inc., 1978.

Claggett, Mary Frances, and Gabriele Lusser Rico. *Balancing the Hemispheres: Brain Research and the Teaching of Writing.* Berkeley: Bay Area Writing Project, University of California, Berkeley, 1980.

Classroom Practices in Teaching English, 1979-80: How to Handle the Paper Load. Edited by Gene Stanford. Urbana, Ill.: National Council of Teachers of English, 1979.

Coles, William. *The Plural I: The Teaching of Writing.* New York: Holt, Rinehart & Winston, Inc., 1978.

The Computer in Composition Instruction. Edited by William Wresch. Urbana, Ill.: National Council of Teachers of English, 1984.

---

[1]To order the publications of the Bay Area Writing Project, write to the Education Business Office, Attn: Publications, 1615 Tolman Hall, University of California, Berkeley, CA 94720, or call (415) 642-8683.

Computers in Composition Instruction. Edited by Joseph Lawlor. Los Alamitos, Calif.: SWRL Educational Research and Development, 1982.

Contemporary Rhetoric: A Conceptual Background with Readings. Edited by W. Ross Winterowd. New York: Harcourt Brace Jovanovich, Inc., 1975.

Copperud, Roy H. *American Usage and Style: The Consensus.* New York: Van Nostrand Reinhold Co., 1980.

Course of Study: A Program Planning Guide for Grades Kindergarten Through Twelve, 1981-84. Hayward, Calif.: Office of the Alameda County Superintendent of Schools, 1981.

Cramer, Ronald. *Writing, Reading, and Language Growth: An Introduction to the Language Arts.* Columbus: Charles E. Merrill Publishing Co., 1978.

Diederich, Paul B. *Measuring Growth in English.* Urbana, Ill.: National Council of Teachers of English, 1974.

Draper, Virginia. *Formative Writing: Writing to Assist Learning in All Subject Areas.* Berkeley: Bay Area Writing Project, University of California, Berkeley, 1979.

Ebbitt, Wilma R., and David R. Ebbitt. *Writer's Guide and Index to English* (Seventh edition). Glenview, Ill.: Scott, Foresman and Co., 1972.

Elbow, Peter. *Writing Without Teachers.* New York: Oxford University Press, Inc., 1973.

Emig, Janet. *The Composing Processes of Twelfth Graders.* Urbana, Ill.: National Council of Teachers of English, 1971.

Encyclopedia of Educational Research (Fifth edition). Edited by Harold Mitzel. New York: Macmillan Publishing Co., Inc., 1982.

Evaluating Writing: Describing, Measuring, Judging. Edited by Charles R. Cooper and Lee Odell. Urbana, Ill.: National Council of Teachers of English, 1977.

Exploring Speaking-Writing Relationships: Connections and Contrasts. Edited by Barry M. Kroll and Roberta J. Vann. Urbana, Ill.: National Council of Teachers of English, 1981.

Fadiman, Clifton, and James Howard. *Empty Pages: A Search for Writing Competence in School and Society.* Belmont, Calif.: Pitman Learning, Inc., 1979.

Fishman, Joshua A. *Sociolinguistics, a Brief Introduction.* Rowley, Mass.: Newbury House Publishers, 1970.

Flower, Linda. *Problem-Solving Strategies for Writing* (Second edition). San Diego, Calif.: Harcourt Brace Jovanovich, Inc., 1985.

Follett, Wilson. *Modern American Usage: A Guide.* Edited and completed by Jacques Barzun. New York: Avenel Books, 1980.

Frank, Marge. *If You're Trying to Teach Kids How to Write, You Gotta Have This Book!* Nashville, Tenn.: Incentive Publications, Inc., 1979.

Friss, Dick. *Writing Class: Teacher and Students Writing Together.* Berkeley: Bay Area Writing Project, University of California, Berkeley, 1980.

Garrison, Roger. *How a Writer Works* (Revised edition). New York: Harper & Row Publishers, Inc., 1985.

Gibson, Walker. *Tough, Sweet, and Stuffy: An Essay on Modern American Prose Styles.* Westport, Conn.: Greenwood Press, 1984.

Gottesman, Julia M. *Peer Teaching: Partner Learning and Small Group Learning.* Downey, Calif.: Office of the Los Angeles County Superintendent of Schools, 1981.

Graves, Donald. *Writing: Teachers and Children at Work.* Portsmouth, N.H.: Heinemann Educational Books, Inc., 1982.

Graves, Donald H. *Balance the Basics: Let Them Write.* New York: Ford Foundation, 1978.

Gray, Stephanie, and Catharine Keech. *Writing from Given Information.* Berkeley: Bay Area Writing Project, University of California, Berkeley, 1980.

Griffith, Marlene. *Writing for the Inexperienced Writer: Fluencey—Shape—Correctness.* Berkeley: Bay Area Writing Project, University of California, Berkeley, 1979.

Grossman, Florence. *Getting from Here to There: Writing and Reading Poetry.* Montclair, N.J.: Boynton/Cook Publishers, Inc., 1982.

Grubb, Mel. *Using Holistic Evaluation.* Encino, Calif.: Glencoe Publishing Co., Inc., 1981.

Hailey, Jack. *Teaching Writing, K—8.* Berkeley: School of Education, University of California, 1978.

Hatfield, Wilbur W. *An Experience Curriculum in English.* A Report of the Curriculum Commission, National Council of Teachers of English. New York: D. Appleton-Century Co., 1935.

An effective writing program treats writing as a process, a concept which regards the act of writing as an interrelated series of creative activities.

Hawkins, Thom. *Group Inquiry Techniques for Teaching Writing.* Urbana, Ill.: National Council of Teachers of English, 1976.

Healy, Mary K. *Using Student Writing Response Groups in the Classroom.* Berkeley: Bay Area Writing Project, University of California, Berkeley, 1980.

Herman, Jerry. *The Tutor and the Writing Student: A Case Study.* Berkeley: Bay Area Writing Project, University of California, Berkeley, 1979.

Holbrook, David. *English for the Rejected.* Cambridge: Cambridge University Press, 1964.

Judy, Stephen N., and Susan J. Judy. *An Introduction to the Teaching of Writing.* Glenview, Ill.: Scott, Foresman & Co., 1981.

Kinneavy, James L. *A Theory of Discourse.* New York: W. W. Norton, 1980.

Kirby, Dan, and Tom Liner. *Inside Out: Developmental Strategies for Teaching Writing.* Montclair, N.J.: Boynton/Cook Publishers, Inc., 1981.

Knoblauch, C. H., and Lil Brannon. *Rhetorical Traditions and the Teaching of Writing.* Montclair, N.J.: Boynton/Cook Publishers, Inc., 1984.

Koch, Carl, and James M. Brazil. *Strategies for Teaching the Composition Process.* Urbana, Ill.: National Council of Teachers of English, 1978.

Krashen, Stephen, and others. *Second Language Acquisition and Second Language Learning.* Hayward, Calif.: The Alemany Press, 1981.

Lanham, Richard. *Revising Prose.* New York: Charles Scribner's Sons, 1979.

Larson, Richard L. *Children and Writing in the Elementary School: Theories and Techniques.* New York: Oxford University Press, 1975.

Loban, Walter. *Language Development: Kindergarten Through Grade Twelve.* Urbana, Ill.: National Council of Teachers of English, 1976.

Macrorie, Ken. *Searching Writing.* Montclair, N.J.: Boynton/Cook Publishers, Inc., 1980.

Macrorie, Ken. *Uptaught.* Rochelle Park, N.J.: Hayden Book Co., Inc., 1970.

Marland, Michael. *Language Across the Curriculum.* Exeter, N.H.: Heinemann Educational Books, Inc., 1977.

Martin, Nancy, and others. *Writing and Learning Across the Curriculum 11-16.* London: Ward Lock Educational, 1976.

The McGraw-Hill Style Manual: A Concise Guide for Writers and Editors. Edited by Marie M. Longyear. New York: McGraw-Hill Book Company, 1983.

McWilliams, Peter A. *The Word Processing Book: A Short Course in Computer Literacy.* Los Angeles: Prelude Press, 1982.

Mellon, John C. *Transformational Sentence-Combining: A Method for Enhancing the Development of Syntactic Fluency in English Composition,* NCTE Research Report No. 10. Urbana, Ill.: National Council of Teachers of English, 1969.

Moffett, James. *Active Voice: A Writing Program Across the Curriculum.* Montclair, N.J.: Boynton/Cook Publishers, Inc., 1981.

Moffett, James. *Teaching the Universe of Discourse.* Boston: Houghton Mifflin Co., 1982.

Moffett, James, and Betty Jane Wagner. *Student-Centered Language Arts and Reading, K—13: A Handbook for Teachers* (Third edition). Boston: Houghton Mifflin Co., 1983.

Mohr, Marian M. *Revision: The Rhythm of Meaning.* Montclair, N.J.: Boynton/Cook Publishers, Inc., 1984.

Muller, Herbert J. *The Uses of English: Guides for the Teaching of English from the Anglo-American Conference at Dartmouth College.* New York: Holt, Rinehart and Winston, Inc., 1967.

Murray, Donald M. *Learning by Teaching: Selected Articles on Writing and Teaching.* Montclair, N.J.: Boynton/Cook Publishers, Inc., 1982.

Murray, Donald. *A Writer Teaches Writing* (Second edition). Boston: Houghton Mifflin Co., 1984.

Myers, Miles. *A Procedure for Writing Assessment and Holistic Scoring.* Urbana, Ill.: National Council of Teachers of English, 1980.

New Directions in Composition Research. Edited by Richard Beach and Lillian Bridwell. New York: The Guilford Press, 1984.

No Better Way to Teach Writing. Edited by Jan Turbill. Portsmouth, N.H.: Heinemann Educational Books, Inc., 1982.

O'Hare, Frank. *Sentence-Combining: Improving Student Writing Without Formal Grammar Instruction.* Urbana, Ill.: National Council of Teachers of English, 1973.

Ponsot, Marie, and Rosemary Deen. *Beat Not the Poor Desk—Writing: What to Teach, How to Teach It, and Why.* Montclair, N.J.: Boynton/Cook Publishers, Inc., 1982.

An effective writing program builds on students' interests and on their reading and oral language experiences.

Popham, Rae Jeane, and Janet Zarem. *Improving Basic Writing Skills.* Los Angeles: Instructional Objectives Exchange, 1978.

Purves, Alan, and others. *Common Sense in Testing in English.* Urbana, Ill.: National Council of Teachers of English, 1975.

Research on Composing: Points of Departure. Edited by Charles R. Cooper and Lee Odell. Urbana, Ill.: National Council of Teachers of English, 1978.

Rhetoric and Composition: A Sourcebook for Teachers and Writers. Edited by Richard Graves. Montclair, N.J.: Boynton/Cook Publishers, Inc., 1984.

Rico, Gabriele L. *Writing the Natural Way: Using Right-Brain Techniques to Release Your Expressive Powers.* Los Angeles: Tarcher, Jeremy p., Inc., 1983.

Schooling and Language Minority Students: A Theoretical Framework. Los Angeles: Evaluation, Dissemination, and Assessment Center, California State University, Los Angeles, 1981.

Schultz, John. *Writing from Start to Finish.* Montclair, N.J.: Boynton/Cook Publishers, Inc., 1982.

Shaughnessy, Mina P. *Errors and Expectations: A Guide for the Teachers of Basic Writing.* New York: Oxford University Press, 1977.

Sherwin, Stephen J. *Four Problems in Teaching English: A Critique of Research.* Scranton, Penn.: International Textbook Co., 1969.

Siegel, Gail, and others. *Sequences in Writing, Grades K—13.* Berkeley: Bay Area Writing Project, University of California, Berkeley, 1981.

Skutnabb-Kangas, Tove. *Language in the Process of Cultural Assimilation and Structural Incorporation of Linguistic Minorities.* Rosslyn, Va.: National Clearinghouse for Bilingual Education, 1979.

Smith, Frank. *Writing and the Writer.* New York: Holt, Rinehart & Winston, Inc., 1982.

Speaking and Writing, K—12: Classroom Strategies and the New Research. Edited by Christopher J. Thaiss and Charles Suhor. Urbana, Ill.: National Council of Teachers of English, 1984.

Start Early for an Early Start: You and the Young Child. Edited by Ferne Johnson. Ann Arbor, Mich.: Books on Demand, 1976.

Stillman, Peter. *Writing Your Way.* Montclair, N.J.: Boynton/Cook Publishers, Inc., 1984.

Strong, William. *Sentence Combining and Paragraph Building.* New York: Random House, Inc., 1981.

Strunk, William, Jr., and E. B. White. *The Elements of Style* (Third edition). New York: Macmillan Publishing Co., Inc., 1979.

Teaching Writing: Essays from the Bay Area Writing Project. Edited by Gerald Camp. Montclair, N.J.: Boynton/Cook Publishers, Inc., 1983.

Teaching Writing Through Technology: A Resource Guide. Chelmsford, Mass.: Northeast Regional Exchange, Inc., 1983.

Theory and Practice in the Teaching of Composition: Processing, Distancing, and Modeling. Edited by Miles Myers and James Gray. Urbana, Ill.: National Council of Teachers of English, 1983.

Tiedt, Iris M. *The Language Art Handbook.* Englewood Cliffs, N.J.: Prentice-Hall, Inc., 1983.

Tiedt, Iris M., and S. Suzanne Bruemmer. *Teaching Writing in K—8 Classrooms: The Time Has Come.* Englewood Cliffs, N.J.: Prentice-Hall, Inc., 1983.

Thonis, Eleanor W. *Literacy for America's Spanish-Speaking Children.* Newark, N.J.: International Reading Association, 1976.

Most recently, researchers have been focusing more on the process of writing itself and less on teacher behavior and writing as a finished product.

Tollefson, Stephen K. *Shaping Sentences: Grammar and Context.* San Diego, Calif.: Harcourt Brace Jovanovich, Inc., 1985.

Van Nostrand, A.D., and others. *Functional Writing.* Boston, Mass.: Houghton Mifflin Co., 1977.

Vygotsky, Lev. *Thought and Language.* Edited by Gertrude Vakar and translated by Eugenia Hanfmann. Cambridge, Mass.: Massachusetts Institute of Technology Press, 1962.

Weathers, Winston. *An Alternate Style: Options in Composition.* Montclair, N.J.: Boynton/Cook Publishers, Inc., 1980.

Weaver, Constance. *Grammar for Teachers: Perspectives and Definitions.* Urbana, Ill.: National Council of Teachers of English, 1979.

What's Going On? Language/Learning Episodes in British and American Classrooms, Grades 4—13. Edited by Mary Barr and others. Montclair, N.J.: Boynton/Cook Publishers, Inc., 1982.

White, Edward M. *Teaching and Assessing Writing.* San Francisco, Calif.: Jossey-Bass, Inc., Publishers, 1985.

The Writer's Mind: Writing as a Mode of Thinking. Edited by Janice N. Hays and others. Urbana, Ill.: National Council of Teachers of English, 1983.

Writing: Don't Leave It in the Classroom. San Jose, Calif.: South Bay Writing Project, San Jose State University, 1985.

Ylvisaker, Miriam. *An Experiment in Encouraging Fluency.* Berkeley: Bay Area Writing Project, University of California, Berkeley, 1980.

Zinsser, William. *On Writing Well: An Informal Guide to Writing Nonfiction* (Revised edition). New York: Harper & Row Publishers, Inc., 1985.

Zinsser, William. *Writing with a Word Processor.* New York: Harper & Row Publishers, Inc., 1983.

Periodicals

Arnold, Lois V. "Writer's Cramp and Eyestrain—Are They Paying Off?" *English Journal,* Vol. 53 (January, 1964), 10—15.

Burns, Hugh. "Pandora's Chip: Concerns About Quality CAI," *Pipeline* (fall, 1981), 15-16.

Christiansen, Mark. "Tripling Writing and Omitting Readings in Freshman English: An Experiment," *College Composition and Communication,* Vol. 16 (May, 1965), 123—124.

Cooper, Charles R. "Research Roundup: Oral and Written Composition," *English Journal,* Vol. 62 (November, 1973), 1,201—1,203.

Cooper, Charles R. "Research Roundup: Oral and Written Composition," *English Journal,* Vol. 63 (September, 1974), 102—104.

Cooper, Charles R. "Research Roundup: Oral and Written Composition," *English Journal,* Vol. 64 (December, 1975), 72—74.

Cummins, James. "Linguistic Interdependence and the Educational Development of Bilingual Children," *Review of Educational Research,* Vol. 49 (spring, 1979), 222—251.

Dieterich, Daniel J. "Composition Evaluation: Options and Advice," *English Journal,* Vol. 61 (November, 1972), 1,264—1,271.

Dressel, Paul, and others. "The Effect of Writing Frequency Upon Essay-Type Writing Proficiency at the College Level," *Journal of Educational Research,* Vol. 46 (December, 1952), 285—293.

Elley, W. B., and others. "The Role of Grammar in a Secondary School English Curriculum," *Research in the Teaching of English,* Vol. 10 (spring, 1976), 5—21.

Giamatti, A. Bartlett. "The Writing Gap," *Yale,* Vol. 34, No. 4 (January, 1976), 16—26.

Gunderson, Doris V. "Research in the Teaching of English," *English Journal,* Vol. 60 (September, 1971), 792—796.

Haynes, Elizabeth F. "Using Research in Preparing to Teach Writing," *English Journal,* Vol. 67 (January, 1978), 82—88.

Heys, Frank, Jr. "The Theme-a-Week Assumption: A Report of an Experiment," *English Journal,* Vol. 51 (May, 1962), 320—322.

Levin, Robert, and Claire Doyle. "The Microcomputer in the Writing/Reading/Study Lab," *T.H.E. Journal* (February, 1983), 77—79, 100.

Marcus, Stephen. "The Muse and the Machine: A Computers and Poetry Project," *Classroom Computer News* (November/December, 1982), 28—31, 82.

Morenberg, M.; D. Daiker; and A. Kerek. "Sentence Combining at the College Level: An Experimental Study," *Research in the Teaching of English,* Vol. 12 (October, 1978), 245—256.

Odell, Lee. "Measuring the Effect of Instruction in Pre-Writing," *Research in the Teaching of English.* Vol. 8 (fall, 1974), 228—240.

Schwartz, Helen J. "A Computer Program for Invention and Feedback." A paper presented at the 1982 Conference on College Composition and Communication in San Francisco on March 19, 1982.

Schwartz, Helen J. "Monsters and Mentors: Computer Applications for Humanistic Education," *College English,* Vol. 44, No. 2 (February, 1982), 141—152.

Stallard, Charles K. "An Analysis of the Writing Behavior of Good Student Writers," *Research in the Teaching of English.* Vol. 8 (fall, 1974), 206—218.

Strom, Ingrid M. *Research in Grammar and Usage and Its Implications for Teaching Writing,* Bulletin of the School of Education, Indiana University, Vol. 36, No. 5 (September, 1960), 1—21.

"Word Processing: How Will It Shape the Student as a Writer?" *Classroom Computer News* (November/December, 1982), 24—27, 74—76.

Wresch, William. "Computers in the English Class: Finally Beyond Grammar and Spelling Drills," *College English,* Vol. 44, No. 5 (September, 1982), 483—490.

"The Writing Gap: Letters," *Yale,* Vol. 34, No. 7 (April, 1976), 24—31.

Index

"People get better at using language when they use it to say things they really want to say to people they really want to say them to, in a context in which they can express themselves freely and honestly."

John Holt

"Who casts to write a living line, must sweat."

Ben Jonson

Selected Publications of the Department of Education

This publication is one of over 650 that are available from the California State Department of Education. Some of the more recent publications or those most widely used are the following:

ISBN	Title (Date of publication)	Price
0-8011-0271-5	Academic Honesty (1986)	$2.50
0-8011-0722-9	Accounting Procedures for Student Organizations (1988)	3.75
0-8011-0272-3	Administration of Maintenance and Operations in California School Districts (1986)	6.75
0-8011-0216-2	Bilingual-Crosscultural Teacher Aides: A Resource Guide (1984)	3.50
0-8011-0238-3	Boating the Right Way (1985)	4.00
0-8011-0275-8	California Dropouts: A Status Report (1986)	2.50
0-8011-0783-0	California Private School Directory, 1988-89 (1988)	14.00
0-8011-0748-2	California School Accounting Manual (1988)	8.00
0-8011-0715-6	California Women: Activities Guide, K—12 (1988)	3.50
0-8011-0488-2	Caught in the Middle: Educational Reform for Young Adolescents in California Public Schools (1987)	5.00
0-8011-0760-1	Celebrating the National Reading Initiative (1989)	6.75
0-8011-0241-3	Computer Applications Planning (1985)	5.00
0-8011-0749-0	Educational Software Preview Guide, 1988-89 (1988)	2.00
0-8011-0489-0	Effective Practices in Achieving Compensatory Education-Funded Schools II (1987)	5.00
0-8011-0041-0	English-Language Arts Framework for California Public Schools (1987)	3.00
0-8011-0731-8	English-Language Arts Model Curriculum Guide, K—8 (1988)	3.00
0-8011-0710-5	Family Life/Sex Education Guidelines (1987)	4.00
0-8011-0289-8	Handbook for Physical Education (1986)	4.50
0-8011-0249-9	Handbook for Planning an Effective Foreign Language Program (1985)	3.50
0-8011-0320-7	Handbook for Planning an Effective Literature Program (1988)	3.00
0-8011-0179-4	Handbook for Planning an Effective Mathematics Program (1982)	2.00
0-8011-0290-1	Handbook for Planning an Effective Writing Program (1986)	2.50
0-8011-0224-3	Handbook for Teaching Cantonese-Speaking Students (1984)	4.50
0-8011-0680-X	Handbook for Teaching Japanese-Speaking Students (1987)	4.50
0-8011-0291-X	Handbook for Teaching Pilipino-Speaking Students (1986)	4.50
0-8011-0204-9	Handbook for Teaching Portuguese-Speaking Students (1983)	4.50
0-8011-0250-2	Handbook on California Education for Language Minority Parents—Chinese/English Edition (1985)	3.25*
0-8011-0737-7	Here They Come: Ready or Not—Report of the School Readiness Task Force (1988)	2.00
0-8011-0712-1	History–Social Science Framework for California Public Schools (1988)	6.00
0-8011-0782-2	Images: A Workbook for Enhancing Self-esteem and Promoting Career Preparation, Especially for Black Girls (1989)	6.00
0-8011-0227-8	Individual Learning Programs for Limited-English-Proficient Students (1984)	3.50
0-8011-0466-1	Instructional Patterns: Curriculum for Parenthood Education (1985)	12.00
0-8011-0208-1	Manual of First-Aid Practices for School Bus Drivers (1983)	1.75
0-8011-0209-X	Martin Luther King, Jr., 1929—1968 (1983)	3.25
0-8011-0358-4	Mathematics Framework for California Public Schools (1985)	3.00
0-8011-0664-8	Mathematics Model Curriculum Guide, K—8 (1987)	2.75
0-8011-0725-3	Model Curriculum for Human Rights and Genocide (1988)	3.25
0-8011-0252-9	Model Curriculum Standards: Grades 9—12 (1985)	5.50

*The following editions are also available, at the same price: Armenian/English, Cambodian/English, Hmong/English, Korean/English, Laotian/English, Spanish/English, and Vietnamese/English.

0-8011-0762-8	Moral and Civic Education and Teaching About Religion (1988)	3.25
0-8011-0229-4	Nutrition Education—Choose Well, Be Well: A Curriculum Guide for Junior High School (1984)	8.00
0-8011-0228-6	Nutrition Education—Choose Well, Be Well: A Curriculum Guide for High School (1984)	8.00
0-8011-0182-4	Nutrition Education—Choose Well, Be Well: A Curriculum Guide for Preschool and Kindergarten (1982)	8.00
0-8011-0183-2	Nutrition Education—Choose Well, Be Well: A Curriculum Guide for the Primary Grades (1982)	8.00
0-8011-0184-0	Nutrition Education—Choose Well, Be Well: A Curriculum Guide for the Upper Elementary Grades (1982)	8.00
0-8011-0230-8	Nutrition Education—Choose Well, Be Well: A Resource Manual for Parent and Community Involvement in Nutrition Education Programs (1984)	4.50
0-8011-0185-9	Nutrition Education—Choose Well, Be Well: A Resource Manual for Preschool, Kindergarten, and Elementary Teachers (1982)	2.25
0-8011-0186-7	Nutrition Education—Choose Well, Be Well: A Resource Manual for Secondary Teachers (1982)	2.25
0-8011-0253-7	Nutrition Education—Choose Well, Be Well: Food Photo Cards (with nutrient composition charts) (1985)	10.00
0-8011-0254-5	Nutrition Education—Choose Well, Be Well: Teaching Materials for Preschool/Kindergarten Curriculum Guide (in color) (1985)	7.50
0-8011-0303-7	A Parent's Handbook on California Education (1986)	3.25
0-8011-0671-0	Practical Ideas for Teaching Writing as a Process (1987)	6.00
0-8011-0309-6	Program Guidelines for Hearing Impaired Individuals (1986)	6.00
0-8011-0258-8	Program Guidelines for Severely Orthopedically Impaired Individuals (1985)	6.00
0-8011-0684-2	Program Guidelines for Visually Impaired Individuals (1987)	6.00
0-8011-0213-8	Raising Expectations: Model Graduation Requirements (1983)	2.75
0-8011-0311-8	Recommended Readings in Literature, K—8 (1986)	2.25
0-8011-0745-8	Recommended Readings in Literature, K—8, Annotated Edition (1988)	4.50
0-8011-0214-6	School Attendance Improvement: A Blueprint for Action (1983)	2.75
0-8011-0189-1	Science Education for the 1980s (1982)	2.50
0-8011-0339-8	Science Framework for California Public Schools (1978)	3.00
0-8011-0354-1	Science Framework Addendum (1984)	3.00
0-8011-0665-6	Science Model Curriculum Guide, K—8 (1987)	3.25
0-8011-0668-0	Science Safety Handbook for California High Schools (1987)	8.75
0-8011-0738-5	Secondary Textbook Review: English (1988)	9.25
0-8011-0677-X	Secondary Textbook Review: General Mathematics (1987)	6.50
0-8011-0781-4	Selected Financial and Related Data for California Public Schools (1988)	3.00
0-8011-0265-0	Standards for Scoliosis Screening in California Public Schools (1985)	2.50
0-8011-0486-6	Statement on Preparation in Natural Science Expected of Entering Freshmen (1986)	2.50
0-8011-0318-5	Students' Rights and Responsibilities Handbook (1986)	2.75
0-8011-0234-0	Studies on Immersion Education: A Collection for U.S. Educators (1984)	5.00

". . . the high forms of literature offer us the only complete, and thus the most responsible, versions of our experience."

Alan Tate

0-8011-0682-6	Suicide Prevention Program for California Public Schools (1987)	8.00
0-8011-0739-3	Survey of Academic Skills, Grade 8: Rationale and Content for Science (1988)	2.50
0-8011-0192-1	Trash Monster Environmental Education Kit (for grade six)	23.00
0-8011-0236-7	University and College Opportunities Handbook (1984)	3.25
0-8011-0237-5	Wet 'n' Safe: Water and Boating Safety, Grades 4—6 (1984)	2.50
0-8011-0194-8	Wizard of Waste Environmental Education Kit (for grade three)	20.00
0-8011-0670-2	Work Experience Education Instructional Guide (1987)	12.50
0-8011-0464-5	Work Permit Handbook for California Public Schools (1985)	6.00
0-8011-0686-9	Year-round Education: Year-round Opportunities—A Study of Year-round Education in California (1987)	5.00
0-8011-0270-7	Young and Old Together: A Resource Directory of Intergenerational Resources (1986)	3.00

Orders should be directed to:

California State Department of Education
P.O. Box 271
Sacramento, CA 95802-0271

Please include the International Standard Book Number (ISBN) for each title ordered.

Remittance or purchase order must accompany order. Purchase orders without checks are accepted only from governmental agencies. Sales tax should be added to all orders from California purchasers.

A complete list of publications available from the Department, including apprenticeship instructional materials, may be obtained by writing to the address listed above or by calling (916) 445-1260.

89 78984

F88-293 (Second printing) 03-0175 300 12-88 15M